Humanities and Organizations in Dialogue

Humanities and Organizations in Dialogue

Hermeneutic Inquiries

Ghislain Deslandes

LEXINGTON BOOKS
Lanham • Boulder • New York • London

Published by Lexington Books
An imprint of The Rowman & Littlefield Publishing Group, Inc.
4501 Forbes Boulevard, Suite 200, Lanham, Maryland 20706
www.rowman.com

86-90 Paul Street, London EC2A 4NE

Originally published in French as *A propos du management et d'un problème plus général*. © Puf, 2020

British Library Cataloguing in Publication Information Available

Library of Congress Cataloging-in-Publication Data

Names: Deslandes, Ghislain, author.
Title: Humanities and organizations in dialogue : hermeneutic inquiries / Ghislain Deslandes.
Description: Lanham : Lexington Books, [2024] | Includes bibliographical references and index.
Identifiers: LCCN 2024021388 (print) | LCCN 2024021389 (ebook) | ISBN 9781666961720 (cloth) | ISBN 9781666961737 (epub)
Subjects: LCSH: Management—Philosophy. | Management—Study and teaching. | Humanities.
Classification: LCC HD30.19 .D474 2024 (print) | LCC HD30.19 (ebook) | DDC 658—dc23/eng/20240523
LC record available at https://lccn.loc.gov/2024021388
LC ebook record available at https://lccn.loc.gov/2024021389

Contents

Acknowledgments

I would particularly like to thank Laurent Faibis, founder of Xerfi Canal, for the fruitful five-year collaboration that accompanied the writing of these fragments. I would also like to thank Paul Garapon, editorial director of the PUF, for his renewed confidence in the publication of this book in English and Lloyd Lewis for his assistance with the translation of this revised version of the text. I would also like to thank Lexington Books and its teams for their support and for the quality of the reviews, which have helped to improve the text that is now available to readers.

Introduction

On Management and a More General Problem

> There is nothing more dangerous for an individual, nothing more paralysing, than a certain gaze fixed on oneself that isolates, through which the history of the world, human life, society—everything, in short—vanishes, and through which, caught in a selfish circle like people suffering from Omphalophobia, one constantly sees only one's own navel. —Sören Kierkegaard, Pap. II A 187, 1837

The meaning of management would appear to be obvious. Essentially, it is an apparatus designed to stimulate collective action and motivate teams, operating within organizations, to become more effective. And indeed, because it has become almost impossible to imagine a world without organizations, we benefit from the effects of management without always being aware of it (in food, transport, health, etc.).

The fact remains, however, that management, which we might assume to be practically and technically devoted to solving organizational problems, has itself become a problem. The terms "burn-out," "brown-out," "eco-anxiety," "great resignation," or "bullshit jobs," for instance, commonly used in the press but originally derived from scientific research, reveal a malaise that is confirmed by the extremely poor general state of motivation at work in Western countries. It is almost as if management disciplines were somehow ill-equipped—even if, in these fields, there is no shortage of "tools," we might even say that there are tools for all tastes[1]—to solve new problems, linked not only to the widespread loss of motivation at work but also to global warming or geostrategic conflicts.

Nevertheless, it would no doubt be excessive to suggest that, in the contemporary field of management sciences, societal issues, to use the accepted term, constitute uncharted territory. In fact, and increasingly over the past ten years or so, research on the theme of "business and society" has proliferated in the form of specialist publications, with the creation of new journals as well as lecture and seminar series for experienced managers (so-called executive education). Concerns about climate change can thus be understood as a matter of risk situation, because businesses can no longer afford to make strategic decisions without first considering the ethical-political consequences for their stakeholders (civilian populations, air quality, suppliers, etc.).

In other words, managers have come to realize that, above and beyond the contemporary difficulties with which they are directly confronted—a crisis of legitimacy, suffering at work, and the rise of datacracy, to name but a few—they also face what we might call "a more general problem."[2] In this sense, companies and human societies are doubly receptive: the future of society is a preoccupation for the organizations, without which its potential disappearance is at stake. As for organizations, they now carry with them a part of our civilization and our future. Can the spheres of the polis and the oikos—the "house," from which all the notions linked to what we call management today originate—the realms of common good and private interests, still live separately? In fact, it seems abundantly clear that management has existed since the dawn of time, contrary to popular belief,[3] and that it would be neither good nor even imaginable for it to disappear as if by magic from our organizations, freeing or "liberating" them from all vertical power structures. But it is equally certain that the impact of contemporary management sometimes seems limited, if not derisory, in terms of solving the problems that our societies must face.[4]

We now need to rethink exactly what it means to manage an organization and in particular, to reassess the immense weight that they have assumed in the course of our lives. They are certainly at the heart of the business and management environment in the strict sense, but their influence extends far beyond that, into the realms of politics, family, and health. We are born in organizations, we die in them, and we spend the time between those two events within their all-encompassing bailiwick. As Rappin rightly points out, we are simultaneously witnessing the "becoming-organization of the world" and the "becoming-world of organizations." Organizations have become the central reality of our world, and the scientific fields known as "business administration," managerial studies or management sciences exist and operate in reference to this reality. From this point of view, management practitioners and researchers might as well be called "organologists" for those who emphasize organizational structures, "organosophers" for those who are interested in the meaning of these structures themselves, or "organoanalysts" for those who describe the psychological mechanisms at work within them.[5]

Now more than ever, we should be asking ourselves what management means, which requires a great deal of interpretation. Managers are indeed first and foremost "interpreting subjects," individuals always in search of meaning (who, in this way, never exhaust what they are interpreting), as well as technicians specializing in organizational management. The obligation to try to understand the truth of organizations is one they are constantly confronted with. By definition, whether in their role of accountant, strategist, or recruiter, they are constantly seeking to understand organizational phenomena and better comprehend their own role as the "drivers of the organization."

So let us begin by temporarily suspending our natural doxic credulity on what we believe management to be—the polysemy of the term is quite obvious, depending on whether we want to consider its technical, scientific, practical, ethical or political character—and let us focus instead on a concept first proposed by Adolphe Blanqui, a forgotten thinker who was nevertheless regarded in the nineteenth century to be "the true creator of management education"[6] and the father of the notion of "industrial revolution."

WHAT IS MANAGEMENT? AN ATTEMPT AT HISTORICAL INTERPRETATION

Brother of the more famous Auguste,[7] member of the Academy of Moral and Political Sciences as well as heir to Jean-Baptiste Say at the Conservatoire des Arts et Métiers, a moderate liberal who grew increasingly perplexed during over the course of his life,[8] this figure in French history worked tirelessly to promote the teaching of management at a time when next to nobody considered it to be a priority.

However, it is interesting to note that Blanqui's idea of management was unusual to say the least. After visiting and commenting on the great world exhibitions of his days, particularly the London one, in a text that had a great impact at the time,[9] he considered that the primary responsibility of management was to ensure beauty and good taste. This clear alternative to governance by numbers (which he was already wary of; see the work of Arena),[10] to use Alain Supiot's expression,[11] was as much linked to the aesthetics of products, as a factor of comparative advantage between nations and the manufacturers themselves, as it was to his own fierce struggle against the terrible working conditions of the time, notably the filth and misery of factories and offices.

If damaging ugliness and fighting against a damaged aesthetics was the first of Blanqui's concerns, developing a know-how with differences was certainly the second.[12] Translation, in Blanqui's view, was not simply a matter of learning modern languages, requiring above all an appreciation of the cultural and philosophical context of a nation, a region, or a trading partner.[13] Finally, Blanqui placed great emphasis on the exemplary nature of "leaders" while advising them to always keep a close eye on technical developments.

Here, then, are the three criteria of judgment for enlightened management, a rare phenomenon indeed in the industrial world of Blanqui's day. They were never far from his mind: in his 1838 Course in Industrial Economics, for example, we find him already wondering about bullshit jobs and the rampant bureaucracy of the early years of the Industrial Revolution:

> We also see many young people completing their education and flocking to the government offices, where they join the ranks of supernumeraries, spending the best years of their youth copying out letters and drawing up reports; and they count themselves lucky if their family connections or the patronage of a well-placed acquaintance should allow them to draw a paltry salary for their efforts. This is how we have gradually sunk into our current bureaucratic morass and why it takes so long for a case to make its way through the dense web of lazy or parasitic employees who, despite spending their lives in these dusty offices, don't know the first thing about administration, public law, modern languages, the arts, or the general interest (249).

This bureaucratic power, whose absurdities Blanqui describes so well, cannot have been far from his thoughts when, as dean of the Ecole Spéciale de Commerce de Paris (ESCP), the oldest surviving management school in the Western world,[14] he drew up the program of studies. On the one hand, there were certainly courses devoted to learning management techniques (especially accounting) and law, whose importance he clearly acknowledged. In addition, there was an important introduction to industrial discoveries, particularly in the field of chemistry, a crucial factor of transformation in the mid-nineteenth century (as artificial intelligence is for contemporary industry). But the program also included a whole series of disciplines entirely separate from the world of management: language learning (apparently Turkish, Arabic, and Persian were all available options in 1828); geography, which was the subject of a specific course; optional courses in literature and art history also feature; and Blanqui himself proposed a seminar on political economy best imagined in the manner described by Francis Démier:

> The industrial economics course was presented as a wealth science course, but fast became a course on social and political science. Over the course of these lectures, the classical liberal framework evolved in several ways. Blanqui drew inspiration from current affairs. He dealt with the question of banks, credit policy, small property, the tax system, customs policy, railway equipment, and insisted on the need to make constant comparisons with what is happening abroad. He himself traveled widely throughout Europe and read the English press attentively. He also urged his students not to be afraid to talk and think about the major issues facing France.[15]

This way of doing things tells us that for Blanqui, business education was part of a broader picture that includes political news and comparisons of national systems. It was not the science of wealth that Blanqui wanted to teach ex cathedra but a new method for appreciating the full complexity of international relations and their daily evolution. Hence the reference to "social and political science," which must provide learners, whether they are functional managers or future entrepreneurs, with knowledge that can enlighten their judgment in situations, from which political and ethical aspects cannot be excluded.

This program, split between technical disciplines on the one hand (accounting/chemistry) and humanities on the other (languages, political economy, and literature), prompted a remark from undersecretary of state Gaston Vidal, on the occasion of the school's centenary, that "business education strikes a harmonious balance between intellectual training and technical preparation, ensuring that an understanding of life's realities in no way tarnishes the disinterested ideal of learning."[16] This is a conclusion that I feel should be rediscovered and redeployed, as I will attempt to demonstrate over the course of this book.

IS ORGANIZING A PHILOSOPHICAL PROBLEM?

After all, who could seriously doubt that the humanities and liberal arts have a fundamental contribution to make to management education? Contemporary organizations and the business models of the future cannot be effectively decoded and analyzed without recourse to ethical, aesthetic, and political concepts. Trying to understand what happens in organizations—or even what happens within what happens—is the first demand made of economic decision makers. Of course, this is not to say that all interpretations are of equal value. It simply acknowledges the fact that our approach to management is necessarily shaped by our interests and disinterests, our passions and our aversions. The humanities can play the role of "tools" in this field, embracing the multitude of ways in which we might interpret the organizational world, which is marked by history, identities and differences.

And yet, the contribution of the humanities to management, which may seem obvious, is far from universally accepted. Positivism still retains a certain prestige in a discipline that essentially seeks causal and measurable explanations for phenomena. And yet, some might say that the interpretive (and "soft") sciences are, by their very nature, the most likely to provide us with information about the diversity of opinions, affects, and ideas that fill the organizational sphere. They also make it possible, when space is given to divergent voices or analyses that conflict on the essentials, to find new avenues of reflexivity, new concepts and newly stimulated imaginative faculties. As John Caputo puts it when discussing Hans-Georg Gadamer,

> with goodwill, there is nothing we cannot discuss, no difference that we cannot put on the table, no distance that cannot at least be brought to words even if it cannot be crossed, no situation in which we have nothing to learn from one another—even if our understanding of each other will always be incomplete.[17]

As in Blanqui's time, humanistic disciplines appear to be returning to the forefront, particularly in the teaching of organizational management. This return is due in particular to the rise of philosophers of science, who are taking an increasing interest in the subject and who are trying to "grasp" the problematic nature of this discipline, which is being taught to a growing number of university students throughout the world (estimated at 20 percent, which is considerable). What interests these philosophers most is the general problem of managing the "philosophical problem" it poses. Their goal: to decipher the business world, "to awaken organizations and ultimately to emancipate the individual by offering him/her a new reflection on the meaning of his/her work and his/her commitment to active life."[18]

By inviting Plato and a few select others to the table of financiers and marketers, the priority is to propose new ways of approaching management, no longer understood only as a "science"—comparable with the "hard" sciences—as it exists today in the university and academic context,[19] but as a political, economic, and social practice that is part of a broader, civilizational project, and as such implies a certain philosophical conception of the human being. From this point of view, if management scientists have made the being of management their object of research, the philosophers of management are primarily concerned with the being of this being, endeavoring to see more clearly, to use Dominique Lecourt's expression, "what is being done in our societies 'in the name of science,' or against it."[20]

In an attempt to grasp this problem, how can adopting a philosophical approach help us to better understand the problematic nature of management and to respond to the unfulfilled expectations it engenders? How can we "manage" differently, taking into account the demands and emergencies of the age? How can we give management the philosophical dimension it seems to lack while at the same time reconstructing management knowledge that has been shaken by profound technological, environmental, and health changes? How can we bolster the critical efforts made in recent years in management sciences, under the label of critical management studies,[21] by mobilizing a creative dimension that often seems to be missing from this approach, as Bruno Latour notes in his famous article "Why has critique run out of stream?"[22] How can we help management theory to finally banish the overbearing influence of the economic sciences, with their scientific mimicry and narrowing of the semantic field, to finally develop its own concepts, and thus enable management practitioners to regain the ability to think and act?

For what do notions such as innovation, transformation, agility, or flexibility mean today without the possibility of measuring them against the latest research in philosophy and the human sciences, and more generally with the work of those who aspire to think the economic world differently than through the sole prism of traditional managerial studies?

The answer proposed here consists in reversing the trend of "chemically pure" research as formulated in management sciences, a discipline usually far removed from those considered as exogenous (law, mathematics, arts, etc.) as well as from current intellectual life, by relying on essays published in recent years.[23] Initially responding to a request from the independent review *Xerfi Canal*,[24] these short texts were composed with the aim of stimulating the reflection of practitioners, consultants, entrepreneurs, and business executives in particular, as well as that of researchers in management, based on the wealth of contemporary intellectual output in the humanities and social sciences. The reading I am proposing is based on these three orientations.

First, this is a book about books, full of thoughts about other thoughts, concerned with establishing a dialogue between management and other analyses of society in general. The project consists of making people discuss works and authors that rarely receive such attention, due to the silo organization of university disciplines, exploring their differences and complementarities.

Second, the selected works present a wide range of subjects connected to societal debates great and small; some of the essays fall into the field of management studies; and in this case, I offer a philosophical and critical reading. Some come from other fields, such as political science or sociology, for example, more or less close cousins of philosophy itself, and so I highlight the potential of these contributions to inspire new perspectives on managerial practice and theory. Some of these essays were written in English, others written in French and then translated, while still others remain untranslated from the language in which they were composed. Those available in translation provide an opportunity for English-speaking readers to acquaint themselves with ideas not widely discussed in their own language.

Finally, these analyses are driven first and foremost by intellectual curiosity and a spirit of discovery, embracing a diverse array of subjects and authors that one might not necessarily group together. Curiosity and imagination are precisely the qualities required to rethink the "ordinary" practice management, to reinvigorate our view of the reality of organizations and their difficulties. These detours from the beaten path, though contemporary humanities, precisely because they exist outside the field which they observe, provide free, singular analyses conducive to challenging some of our most stubborn professional certainties.

We could easily have chosen to present these inquiries in a wilfully disordered manner, as a sort of hypertext in which all the writings taken separately would have constituted a possible point of access to the rest of the corpus. This is not the approach adopted here. Instead, I felt that the priority was to provide an overview of what I call in the first section "the limits of negotium"[25] (i.e., the customary practices of business that no longer make sense without a more general diagnosis of the world in which they operate). Faced with the pitfalls of the present time, there is every reason to believe that the familiar discourses on leadership, and the prevailing "dataism"—reducing the world and human life to a flow of data—will not be capable of rising to the technological and ecological challenges facing economic and political decision makers. This is the subject of the second chapter. However, reintroducing a dose of the "humanities" into the practice of management, which has gradually shied away from such pursuits, could be the best way to tackle the socioeconomic and ecological challenges that are currently shaking up our collective destiny, as we shall see in the third and final chapter.

NOTES

1. For example, R. Juët, *The Manager's Toolbox. 50 Practical Sheets for Managing Your Team*, third edition (Paris: Dunod, 2017).
2. To borrow the expression employed by Gilles Deleuze in a famous 1977 article on the "new philosophers" ("On the new philosophers, and a more general problem," in *Deux régimes de fous. Texts and interviews 1975–1995* (Éditions de Minuit, 2003), 127–34).
3. G. Deslandes, *Critique de la condition managériale*, PUF, 2016.
4. A few recent events on the economic scene, such as the repeated conflicts at the SNCF or, more anecdotally, the episode of the torn shirt of Air France's human resources director—a striking incident that took place October 5, 2015—have shown that people no longer want to be managed (governed?) as in the past.
5. G. Deslandes and J. P. Bouilloud, "De quoi notre métier est-il le nom? Perspectives pour un débat," *Revue française de gestion 309*, no. 2 (2023): 85–99.
6. A. Renouard, *History of the Ecole Supérieure de Commerce (1820–1898)*, Union amicale des anciens élèves, 79 Avenue de la République (Paris, 1898), 199.
7. Arguably the main figure of French revolutionary socialism of that time.
8. These paragraphs are taken from a study published in English in *European Management Review*: G. Deslandes, 2019: *"European management teaching and research: Reflections on the life and work of A. Blanqui" 38*, no. 3 (June 2020): 357–66.
9. A. Blanqui, *Lettres sur l'Exposition universelle de Londres* (Paris Capelle Libraire-éditeur, 1851).
10. R. Arena, «Adolphe-Jérôme Blanqui, 1798–1854. Un historien de l'économie aux préoccupations sociales», in Y. Breton and M. Lutfalla, eds., L'*économie politique en France au xixe siècle* (Paris: Economica, 1991).

11. A. Supiot, *Governance by numbers. Courses at the Collège de France, 2012–2014,* Institut d'Études avancées de Nantes/Fayard, 2015. See also Barbara Cassin, *Derrière les grilles. Sortons du tout-évaluation* (Mille et Une Nuits, 2014).

12. See Barbara Cassin, *Éloge de la traduction : compliquer l'universel*, Pluriel, 2022.

13. Blanqui remarked, for example, in his best-known work (*Des classes ouvrières en France pendant l'année 1848,* Paris, Pagnère Libraire): "I found Africa quite different from the flattering or sinister paintings by which we have become accustomed to judging it," before adding: "it is not the same everywhere; it is not even a unified whole" (2–3). Another example: "One would therefore get a very false idea of the condition of the worker in France, if one could confuse in the same category those of the North and the South, those of Lille and Rouen with the workers of Marseille and Bordeaux" (32).

14. ESCP Business School celebrated the bicentenary of its creation in 2019. By way of comparison, HEC was founded in 1881, the Ecole Supérieure de Commerce de Marseille in 1872, and Harvard Business School in 1908.

15. Francis Démier, «Blanqui, Adolphe (1798–1854). Professeur d'Économie industrielle (1834–1854)», in *Les professeurs du Conservatoire national des Arts et Métiers. Dictionnaire biographique, 1794–1955*, vol. 1: A–K, (Paris: Institut national de Recherche pédagogique [INRP], 1994), 185–94.

16. ESCP, *Centennial Bulletin*, 617.

17. J. Caputo, *Hermeneutics and Information. Facts and Interpretation of the Age of Information*, 111.

18. "Who are we?," *philonomist.com*, February 22, 2020. In a recent special issue of the *Rue Descartes* magazine, which historically has not been much inclined to deal with this subject, a group of authors also proposed "Philosophical Variations on the Question of Management" (*Rue Descartes*, Collège International de philosophie, 2017/1, n° 91), available at https://www.cairn.info/revue-rue-descartes-2017-1.htm, offering new analyses of the economic-management environment as a linguistic and symbolic space.

19. "Management Sciences," section 06 of the CNU (National Council of Universities).

20. D. Lecourt, «Pourquoi enseigner la philosophie et l'histoire de sciences dans les cursus scientifiques», *Rue Descartes 41*, no. 3 (2003): 105–8, doi :10.3917/rdes.041.0105.

21. M. Alvesson and H. Willmott, eds., *Studying Management Critically* (Londres: Sage, 2003).

22. http://www.bruno-latour.fr.

23. At least for the vast majority of them.

24. https://www.xerficanal.com.

25. I use the Latin term here to refer to business and trading activities, as opposed to *otium*, which refers to leisure activities, considered at the time to be the activity par excellence.

Chapter 1

The Limits of *Negotium*

The aim of this first chapter is to take a fresh look at management, its meaning and its limits, stepping outside the established disciplines of management studies with the help of a corpus of essays in the human and social sciences. Admittedly, since the first works of Alvesson and Willmott in 1992,[1] there has been a growing critical tendency in the management literature, which has continued to develop at the institutional level. But in this study, I have chosen to focus on works by historians (Todeschini, Muller, Godin), sociologists (Graeber, Bouilloud, Lahire), and philosophers (Musso, Rappin, Rovère, Rey, Chrétien, Alizart, Perry) who are not, strictly speaking, specialists in management studies. The fifteen or so works presented here, which do not deal with the question of management as such, nevertheless offer an unusual insight into aspects that raise questions about the practice and theory of management sciences. Existing on the fringes of management research, without devoting particular attention to it, each of these essays engages in its own way with some of the most problematic aspects of the discipline, from the reputation of merchants since the Middle Ages to the theological origins of industry and the disproportionate importance attached to numbers by organizations . . . to the point of making it impossible for managerial thinking to extract itself from its "calculocratic" prerogatives.

MANAGERIALISM IS NOT A HUMANISM

In many ways, these analyses encourage us to ask why today's managers deprive themselves of the imaginative resources that would enable them to reconnect with their deepest motivations. If the job of manager no longer inspires us, it is precisely because our imaginative resources need a recharge, with new premises better suited to the present time. Jacques Bouveresse discussed this difficulty in a text published six years after his election to the Collège de France, during a lecture delivered at HEC and titled "Can managers have ideals?"[2] Drawing upon some of his favorite authors, notably Karl Krauss and Robert Musil, he underlined the gulf that has opened up over time between intellectuals (supposedly capable of ideals) and merchants, who claim to be incapable of inventing anything other than a "realistic" world (i.e., one exclusively devoted to money, commerce, and industry).[3]

Bouveresse was intent on challenging this false opposition to offer the budding managers in the audience a radical alternative to the disenchantment that always results from the tyrannical separation between the establishment of so-called facts (of management), elevated to the rank of a single ideal, and the expressive potential of an imaginary capable of stepping outside this paradigm, an ideal that we might describe as "humanist." However, in contrast to the optimism that emanates from the conclusion of his text, which sees it as a challenge not to reconcile but to bring into tension, the need for rationality and functionality with the need for humanity that he glimpses through philosophical work, the contemporary essays selected here underline the limits of these hopes and the long road that remains to be traveled.

How can we rethink the categories of the economy by dissociating them from their theological past? How can we avoid the retroactive functionalism of organizations and the resulting state of permanent exception? In short, can organizations escape from the managerialism that pushes them, as Alvesson and Spicer would have it, ever deeper into "functional stupidity?" Unfortunately, the prevailing calculocracy that has taken hold of so many companies—as several authors point out, evoking the growing weight of numbers in the functioning of the economy—seems ill-equipped to nurture the emergence of a new imaginary centered on affectio societatis rather than on the tyranny of dashboards.

Moreover, as Bouveresse explains in his remarks on Novalis, "egoism, which could be thought to be the only greatness that lends itself to measurement, calculation, forecasting and rational management, is in reality an essence without measure, without limits and without rules."[4] This is precisely the point made by critiques of governance by numbers, because numbers generally provide only a partial, impoverished view of the complexity of reality. This is not to say that accountability, identifying needs, or projecting numerical objectives are necessarily problematic: quantitative evaluation is an inevitable criterion for steering organizations. The problem is that it tends to become the only criterion, reducing the historical and cultural depth of organizations to a sequence of numbers, and subjecting them to a model of rationality concerned exclusively with quantification—as if we were living in an economic world in which quality is a mere emanation from the hegemonic force of quantity and whence all sense of perspective has long since departed.

Of course, contemporary organizations do their best to respond to such reproaches, multiplying their efforts in favor of creativity and innovation, concepts that have been much studied in sociology and history and deserve more attention. Other, more philosophical perspectives have argued that the best way to escape from managerialism[5] is to take a step back, or even to escape the stress of professional life, by championing procrastination, putting otium before negotium. This is a point that would have frightened Fredrick Winslow Taylor, the American engineer to whom managerialism owes so much; he observed that the aim of the scientific organization of work was precisely to fight against laziness, its greatest enemy.

The work presented here on the notions of organizational creativity and innovation shows that neither is a panacea, but first and foremost, they deserve a historical and critical treatment. The shift in management thinking operated by these contributions leads us to reconsider not only the dream function to which managers might aspire, but also the role of poetic activity and of "negative capacities" as first expressed by the English poet John Keats. A simple question comes to mind, which we shall endeavor to answer later on: "is it not time to teach managers poetry?"

The Merchants in the Temple: What Status for Wealth?

Giacomo Todeschini, *Les Marchands et le Temple: La société chrétienne et le cercle vertueux de la richesse du Moyen Âge à l'Epoque moderne*[6] (Albin Michel, 2017).

At the very top of the social hierarchy: the philosophers and the leaders of the city; in the middle: the warriors; at the very bottom of the social ladder: the merchants and the craftsmen. This, in a simplified version, is the hierarchical organization that Plato proposed to his contemporaries: business was not held in high regard.

With the historian Giacomo Todeschini, we learn that it was in the Middle Ages that the social revaluation of the figure of the merchant took place, a profession that since the Greeks had been in search of legitimacy on the moral level. Driving the merchants out of the temple and pointing out how difficult it would be for a rich man to enter the Kingdom of God, Jesus also played a role in the social downgrading of merchants. But in Europe, from the eleventh through to the fifteenth centuries, the legitimacy of commercial activities and the use of wealth—the question of a "public" good, for example—were all widely discussed and scrutinized, particularly by theologians. A good merchant is one who demonstrates commendable intent. Then he shows himself capable of judging his own actions on the principle of restitution, offsetting the profits of usury with donations to worthy causes. Finally, to be respectable, or even venerable, the accumulation of wealth and earthly goods must somehow be related to the common good. Immobilized wealth is ignominious; invested in what we would call today "the productive apparatus," it becomes an estimable value. In short, without public utility, money is a dead weight.

In his introduction to the French edition, Thomas Piketty writes that "this is an attempt to trace those forgotten ethical, religious or charismatic influences that were truly, structurally important to the expression of economic meaning in the pre-modern Era." The Middle Ages thus appeared to have played an underestimated role in the construction of our contemporary economic categories. The influence of this age of mankind is evident with regard to the economic vocabulary we use: administration, value, capital, investment, use, compensation, all were common currency in the theological debates of the period. Unbeknownst to us, the words we use are imbued with a long tradition of sacred associations inherited from another time, an imaginary that is all the more difficult to challenge today because it is firmly rooted in our unconscious. This is undoubtedly the reason why certain ways of thinking persist, even though they no longer correspond to the present time.

Regarding the subtitle of the book, one might wonder what remains of Christianity, or of virtue, in the contemporary economic world. At that time, "indifference" to money was considered an important virtue. Hence the words of a medieval bishop quoted by Todeschini, echoing the Epistle to the Philippians: "All can have much, but only those who are not corrupted by abundance know how to have much." I am not certain that the relationship between the sacred and the profane, the calculable and the incalculable, money and the absolute, could be formulated with such subtlety and resolution today. Another question presents itself: Is possessing things "as if we didn't possess them" still an acceptable proposition, and if so, what meaning should it have in contemporary society?

The "Industrial Religion": From the Monastery to the Factory

Pierre Musso, *La religion industrielle. Monastères, manufactures, usines*[7] (Fayard, 2017).

In *The Future of an Illusion*, Freud expresses himself in the following terms:

> If you want to abolish religion from our European culture, that can only happen as a result of a different doctrinal system, and from the outset that system would assume, in its own defence, all the psychological characteristics of religion: the same sanctity, rigidity, intolerance, the same ban on thought.

For Pierre Musso, this other system of doctrine has a name: industry. When we talk about industry, what comes to mind, if not religion? This long, well-documented investigation, illustrated with old engravings and paintings, shows that, from the monastery to the manufactory through to the modern factory, we can trace not the secularization of religion but, instead, an unacknowledged religious mode of functioning that has shaped industry.

In defense of this thesis, which is singular to say the least, the author relies in particular on the work of Pierre Legendre who, in *Dominium Mundi*, showed that a discourse founded on industry and management is a central element of faith for Western man. Since the eleventh century, this discourse has been built up gradually in numerous phases, intensified since the French Revolution, which provide the structure and material for Pierre Musso's investigation.

But several theses are at work in this book. The most easily refutable among them is the idea that this new faith in industrial religion masks a "new techno-scientific Christianity." The author sees in it the extension of a Christian figure of incarnation, as if the "head body of the manager" and the body of the worker-Christ, to use his expressions, were the new pastors of this postmodern cult; as if the company were in some way the last avatar of Romano-Christianity. To that we must surely respond that, far from being connected to any notion of Christian theology, the managerial revolution went in the opposite direction. The question "why" was eliminated altogether, at the expense of "how." Musso artfully quotes Gilles Deleuze, an author who can hardly be accused of Christian proselytism: "We are strict functionalists," Deleuze stated in an interview with Claire Parnet; "what interests us is how something works, how it functions as a machine."

It is worth noting, however, that this genealogy of industrial religion, coming from one of the leading specialists in the thought of Henri de Saint-Simon, is convincing on a point of prime importance: "we cannot think about management using the categories derived from sacred thought, which are of a different order. Just think of the quasi-theological virtues we know as performance, governance, and so forth. . . . Just as there is a hermeneutics of religious texts, a critical art of interpretation, there must also be a critical art of managerial 'normativity.'"

This critical and historical perspective is what management sciences need now more than ever, to be considered not as high-performance computer-assisted techniques, but as an ethical and political practice that recognizes its constraints to better overcome them.

Is It Possible to Avoid Total Bureaucratization?

David Graeber, *The Utopia of Rules: On Technology, Stupidity, and the Secret Joys of Bureaucracy* (Melville House, 2015).

Has the combination of liberalism and technology kept all its promises? For David Graeber, there is no doubt that it has not, at least on one point, which is the staggering increase in red tape, which spares absolutely no one. Whether we are citizens, taxpayers, parents, employees, or entrepreneurs, whoever we are, we cannot escape it: piles of protocols, forms, questionnaires, and surveys constantly cry out for our attention. Graeber, an anthropologist and LSE professor who sadly passed away in September 2020, and who considered himself to be close to the anarchist and libertarian traditions, argues that we have entered into the "era of total bureaucratization." This is akin to the realization of Max Weber's fears: a steel cage in which all forms of nuance, subtlety, and finesse will soon have disappeared.

During each new presidential campaign, we are treated to fresh homilies about the absolute necessity of simplifying administrative procedures, for example, when founding a new business. We also hear plenty of promises to finally cut out the time wasted filling in superfluous documents, monopolizing energy that could otherwise be devoted to economic development. The most liberal-minded of our politicians are, moreover, the first to denounce this administrative stranglehold on economic life, which is the bearer of all evils.

David Graeber's central hypothesis, however, is that market rationality and the continuous increase in administrative pressure go hand in hand. This unexpected alliance is not accidental: the author points out that if certain professional associations, employers' unions, banks, or large international companies are constantly calling for a relaxation of the legal framework, they generally forget that this framework was often established at their own request, to preserve their interests, as defended by the lobbyists and lawyers charged with negotiating on their behalf. And the author points out two elements that are all too often overlooked: on the one hand, the American society, more bureaucratic now than it has ever been, is not a good fit for the idea that Americans have of themselves; on the other hand, that the transformation of the Soviet and Maoist ultra-bureaucracies into radical capitalist societies took place without major administrative difficulties, because the cohabitation of an iron-fisted bureaucracy and frenzied capitalism seems to have been achieved without damaging either. The author denounces, as do so many of us, the pressure that creeping bureaucracy places on our freedoms. Basically, bureaucracies "set imperatives by swearing that they are reasonable; then they discover that they are not; then they conclude that it is not the imperatives that are the problem, but the individual inadequacy of each human being."

In fact, we are not all equal in the face of the cumbersome system: some do not do as well as others. Consider the example of the movie *Mammuth*[8] in which a former worker who follows the advice of a pension fund when advised to "go to the site" to retrieve his old pay slips and sort out his pension rights: he reaches his former workplace, with great difficulty, only to find that the factory has closed and that nothing and no one is able to provide the slightest response to his requests.

This book tackles an almost universal problem in a striking manner, not hesitating to draw on real-life examples and reminding us above all that humanity, whatever its definition, deserves better than spending its time filling out forms.

Coping with Numberization

Olivier Rey, *Quand le monde s'est fait nombre*[9] (Stock, 2016).

Numberization, quantophrenia,[10] calculocracy: we are constantly inventing new words to describe the growing importance of numbers in our society and in our companies. Governance by numbers no longer seems to have any limits, because even nation-states are now bound by international agreements that dictate the terms of their public deficit.

This rise in numbers finds a formidable amplifier in the increased amount of computer data in circulation. If we look at the latest ranking of the ten "professions of the future," using the method proposed by the American site careercast.com, half of these professions are directly concerned with figures: statisticians, computer analysts, scientists specialising in data processing, mathematicians, and computer developers. Among the maths bods only traders, soon to be replaced by algorithms, will be the big losers in this evolution.

In his latest essay, mathematician and philosopher Olivier Rey invites us to reflect upon how numbers came to achieve such dominance. A specialist in "nonlinear partial differential equations" and the thought of Ivan Illich, two fields of knowledge that would appear to be far removed from each other, Rey sets out to demonstrate how quantification and statistical science have become increasingly important in the field of political and economic decision making.

Above all, he states that this position was not built in a day. Some indigenous peoples of the Amazon basin, particularly the Pirahas, saw no need to count beyond two. For the Munduruku, another Amazonian culture, there was no point in counting more than five . . . because then began, the author writes, "the rule of the many." In fact, it was only after the seventeenth century, when the separation between the humanities and the sciences did not yet exist, that statistics emerged as a field in its own right.

Contrary to what one might expect from a philosopher, Rey is in many ways a defender of statistics and the science of numbers. He quotes, for example, Fénelon who, in *Directions for the Conscience of King*, poses a clear question, "What would we think of a shepherd who did not know the number of his flock?" Indeed, he considers that decision making always requires access to figures and that this approach is indispensable for those who claim to want to govern the world.

Nevertheless, Rey rarely misses an opportunity to mock the misuse of figures. He quotes, for example, the playwright Eugène Labiche and his derisive remarks on the fashion for statistics in the nineteenth century: "Statistics, Madame, is a modern and positive science," says one of his characters, secretary of a hypothetical statistical society in Vierzon. "It sheds light on the most obscure facts. Thus, thanks to laborious research, we have recently come to know the exact number of widows who passed on the Pont-Neuf during the year 1860."

In some respects, therefore, this book attempts to limit the scope of datacracy. Admittedly, the "reality of numbers" does not correspond exactly to reality, and their supposed truth, in terms of what we feel within ourselves, is often useless and vain. But from another point of view, Rey reconciles us with the necessity of their existence, because "it is (precisely) our respect for the singularity of each person that obliges us to stick to that which can be measured." This carries echoes of a topic discussed by some of the great philosophers, not least Montaigne and Pascal. The law of numbers is a strength, which can compensate for our own weak points when it comes to deciding human affairs. But this strength does not have the power to tell us who we are, how we live, and what we experience. It falls to us to avoid the temptation, a profoundly dangerous temptation at that, of elevating numbers to sacred status.

The Tyranny of Performance Indicators

Jerry Z. Muller, *The Tyranny by Numbers* (Princeton, NJ: Princeton University Press, 2018).

How do we access the "truth" of organizations today? By the most direct route available: quantified evaluation. The belief that it is numbers, and only numbers, that can provide access to the truth of organizations has spread like wildfire across the global economy, to the point that data have become the only legitimate yardstick for judging the health of companies. The American historian Jerry Muller calls this trend "the tyranny of metrics."

In this book, Muller denounces the excesses—and only the excesses—of the cult of calculability that has imposed itself in many fields, especially commercial companies, but also universities and hospitals. He highlights the many organizational absurdities engendered by this calculocratic obsession and the way in which certain measurement systems end up obtaining the opposite result to what they originally intended.

He cites an example from the United Kingdom: the Department of Health and Social Care began penalizing public hospitals where A&E waiting times exceeded four hours. Very quickly, the statistics showed an improvement in results, and the operation was deemed a success . . . before it was realized that the emergency services had started making patients wait in ambulances so that they were not counted in the waiting rooms.

He also gives the example of board members of large American companies who, so concerned with ensuring the accuracy of their financial statements since the implementation of the Sarbanes-Oxley Act on the reform of accounting for U.S. listed companies, have simply forgotten to focus on their corporate strategy because they no longer have enough time.

Muller also provides numerous examples—particularly from the United States, where the collective unconscious is convinced of its relative imperviousness to the risk of bureaucratic overload (as David Graeber also noted)—that illustrate the inconsistencies of this evaluative passion. This frenzy has three major components: the belief that figures can replace personal judgment and experience; the idea that the transparency of figures strengthens the credibility and seriousness of the organizations that put them in place; finally, the vague but tenacious feeling that professionals are generally motivated only by the rewards, particularly the bankable rewards, available for carrying out their missions.

Thus, we have come to measure relentlessly, without really knowing what we are measuring, to such an extent that the cost of these additional measurements exceeds the potential savings they are supposed to bring. It is as if the tyranny of measuring instruments were designed to gloss over the immeasurable, to distract us from considering what really counts, and to prevent us from producing any form of novelty. For, as Muller puts it, "what is not yet known cannot be measured."

This state of affairs has some lessons for managerial practice itself. The author points out that quantophrenia can be partly explained in environments where extrinsic rewards are the main motivating factor, or in the case (and this is not incompatible) where trust between the parties is reduced to a bare minimum. On the other hand, when people consider their profession to be a vocation, and expect to derive personal satisfaction from it (nurses, researchers, doctors, journalists, etc.), then a strictly quantitative approach on the part of management can have tragic consequences for the other criteria that define the health of an organization: reputation, customer satisfaction, employee commitment, and so on—in short, every aspect of their affectio societatis.[11]

Despite it all, the incalculable is still present in organizations in various forms: the identity of individuals, good manners, or simply keeping one's word are striking examples of this. The challenge ahead is to define a new "biodiversity" of evaluation.

Heavenly Computing, a New Impasse for Management?

Mark Alizart, *Informatique céleste*,[12] "Perspectives critiques" (Paris: PUF, 2017).

During the 1950s, engineers at IBM France were looking for an appropriate French translation for the term computer. They asked philologist Jacques Perret, who advised them to avoid the word combinateur, which they had initially thought of, because of its depreciative association with its derivative, the term "combine." They thus selected ordinateur, an old Latin suddenly brought up to date, whose primary meaning was the capacity reserved for God alone of setting the world in order. "Deus Ordinator," as per the *Littré* dictionary: "God who orders the world."

For the philosopher Mark Alizart, this etymological root is no coincidence, because computer science is not a human invention but, rather, a natural phenomenon, a property of life. It was not the word that came first, but the number. In a way, lines of code can be said to "already exist" in nature, and everything they contain can be transposed into information, which, in its most contemporary expression, is essentially synonymous with computer science. This is a vision of "celestial computing," the title to this essay, which seems determined to reconcile numbers and letters by showing that it is computing that represents the culmination of human thought, much more so than philosophy.

The author contends that thinking is, first and foremost, a matter of calculating and learning dynamically, which is something that machines are capable of doing. Modern computers operate on the same principle as our own mental processes (i.e., in a nonlinear manner). This is an idea that first emerged in the 1950s at the Macy Conferences, kick-starting the development of cybernetics, a research program that sought to unify all the mental sciences into a coherent whole. At the time, authors such as Norbert Wiener were already trumpeting a great structuralist transformation of our conception of the world. This intellectual project is that of a bygone era, as Jean-Pierre Dupuy makes clear in *Aux origines des sciences cognitives* (La Découverte, 2005), demonstrating the limitations of this engineering-inspired worldview that reduces thought to a process without a subject.

But let us not delude ourselves. The ontological assumption that Being is information has prevailed in management for decades. A regular participant in the Macy Conferences, Herbert Simon, one of the most influential authors in management sciences, declared in 1965 that "in the space of twenty years, machines will be capable of performing all the tasks that men can do." To put it plainly, computers were already for him living, autonomous organisms, almost bodies, as if endowed with a "self" (the Greek term for which is "auto," as Alizart reminds us).

Faced with this idea, new to philosophy but already very common in management (Gilbreth, Taylor's disciple, wrote that the objective of management is to "lead men to behave like machines as much as possible"), should we not be putting our faith in theoretical models that give a central place to subjective interiority and human affectivity? "What part of us feels pleasure?" Pascal asked. "Is it the hand, is it the arm, is it the flesh, is it the blood?" No, it is life that feels itself and is at the heart of contemporary debates about work, where individuals want to be appreciated for who they are: calculating machines at times, perhaps, but above all beings endowed with sensitivity who enjoy, who suffer, who savor. This consideration will be of central importance to any future efforts to develop a more enlightened, more humane, and more joyful vision of management. More celestial, even.

Management in the Face of Obsolete Cybernetic Schemes

Baptiste Rappin, *Heidegger et la question du management*[13] (Nice: Ovadia, 2015).

"Don't forget to give us your feedback," "send me your corrective action plan": two sentences frequently encountered within organizations. Establishing initial objectives, setting up an action plan and then establishing indicators of success or failure, taking corrective action according to the results obtained, this is the usual cycle that informs most management systems. Such recursive and so-called original build/measure/learn type processes, the three key words of lean start-ups devoted to minimizing uncertainty, are merely the umpteenth incarnation of the same feedback control scheme that has been imposed on management for decades.

We can precisely date the appearance of these notions of feedback, learning, modeling, or coding, which are today unavoidable for anyone working in a company or even in a public administration. However, it is not generally known that they all originated from the Macy Conferences, held from the mid-1940s onward in the United States. These scientific seminars are today considered to be the point of origin of the cybernetics movement, devoted to unifying all fields of knowledge around information sciences.

If there is one field where this unification has occurred, it is management. As Baptiste Rappin has demonstrated—and particularly this one, where he engages with the thought of German phenomenologist Martin Heidegger—it is the cybernetic notion of feedback that presides over the development of almost all management disciplines: in particular, control, strategy, and human resources management. Baptiste Rappin describes several examples of functional structures in the form of spirals or reels, such as the Deming wheel or Kaplan and Norton's balanced scorecard, which laid the groundwork for the countless iterations that have since emerged from the management literature. The idea is to initiate a circular movement each time, which returns to its original position after having gone through a series of stages.

The idea behind this roundabout and integral logic is twofold: the first is to fight against the uncertainty of life by putting in place a perpetual learning mechanism, to which Rappin replies that management is indeed a permanent state of exception.

The second idea, linked to the first, is to uphold a principle of equivalence between the brain and electronics. This is precisely where Heidegger comes in, when he states that "in the representation of the world by cybernetics, the difference between machines and living beings is (purely and simply) abolished." Between the two, information, which has become a general equivalent, is supposed to be capable of making man and machine progress together, through iterative processes.

What are we to make of it all? In the meantime, emotional consciousness has disappeared, human affectivity appears to have been swept away in the flow of communication, to the extent that living work has all but disappeared. The retroactive functionalism of management unfolds, shedding all human energy that is not immediately productive. In short, as Rappin states, "the flesh of the employee has disappeared," that of the manager, too, and her ability to meditate her own work with it. Therefore, at a time when more and more organizational theorists seem to be calling for the emergence of a more humane management, is it not finally time to question the old-world thought patterns of cybernetics?

The Paradox of "Functional Stupidity"

Mats Alvesson and André Spicer, *The Stupidity Paradox. The Power and Pitfalls of Functional Stupidity at Work* (London: Profile Book, 2016).

Do we still leave room for the expression of human intelligence in bureaucratic organizations? Has "Just do it!" become much more than the slogan of a sports equipment manufacturer, now serving as the general modus operandi for many contemporary companies? These are the key questions posed by two influential authors in contemporary management studies, Mats Alvesson and André Spicer.

They denounce a phenomenon of "functional stupidity" that, despite the declarations of principle of companies still fond of "science parks," innovation zones, and knowledge clusters, corresponds to an inclination to reduce the field of vision of employees. Functional stupidity reaches its apogee when agents are capable of doing their jobs without ever asking the slightest question about their raison d'être. For Alvesson and Spicer, this phenomenon primarily affects the most highly educated employees, and herein lies a striking paradox: you must be relatively intelligent to become functionally stupid.

According to the authors, this phenomenon operates in three stages: first, not questioning what is fashionable, the doxa, the common idea. One begins to lack personal reflexivity; one shows oneself to be incapable of doubting the dominant beliefs. The second stage corresponds to ignoring the reasoning behind actions in favor of blind respect for hierarchical order, tacit conventions, even organizational taboos. In the third stage, people stop asking themselves about the consequences of their actions beyond their own perimeter. They thus restrict their reasoning capacities to the strict minimum (i.e., to the technical aspect of their past and present actions).

Of course, the authors are aware that reflexive thinking of a critical nature can be misunderstood. And if managers operate at this reduced level, it is because they have an interest in it. Isn't it better to implement decisions without flinching than to constantly question their relevance and meaning? By cultivating functional stupidity, explain Alvesson and Spicer, organizations hope to avoid the cost of questioning existing patterns.

In the short term, functional stupidity offers certain guarantees of stability and efficiency. But in the long term, wishful thinking, sterile fashion effects, unexamined imitation of competitors, blind pursuit of dubious objectives, especially from an ethical point of view, can have tragic consequences. The authors cite the example of Nokia, the mobile phone manufacturer brought low by its own Symbian software, a monumental failure that no one in the company was willing to acknowledge, because the corporate culture at the time forbade the expression of the slightest negative thought. Suppressing awareness of problems, or problems of conscience, has never solved any problems.

Challenging our current opinions and being ready to justify our actions are proof of the intellectual maturity that companies need. Managers are not only there to coerce and imitate, and then take the glory; their job is to innovate and imagine new business models. In this department, stupidity cannot help.

The Heuristics of Stupidity

Jean-François Marmion (under the direction of), *The Psychology of Stupidity* (translated by Liesl Schillinger) (New York: Penguin, 2020).

Throughout our lives, there will always be occasions on which we find ourselves jabbing repeatedly at the lift button when we are late for an appointment; asking someone who is crying how they are doing; shaking the dice more vigorously in the hop of rolling a six, and all without acknowledging that this behavior is foolish. It is the lot of fools that they never really ask themselves whether they are fools. For the rest of us, it may well be useful and timely to better understand the little stupidities of our daily behavior, if necessary, to remedy them.

This is what Serge Ciccotti proposes in particular, in his contribution on, one hardly dares type the words, "the scientific study of morons." He identifies some of the psychological biases studied in scientific research articles and offers a very enlightening synthesis of them, encompassing the illusion of control, which gives a plausible explanation for the examples cited above, strategies for safeguarding self-esteem, the egocentric bias reached by those who "failed because they work with a bunch of idiots," or the negativity bias, when we systematically accuse others of being responsible for the glasses or keys we have just misplaced—in short, all the various forms of bias that can explain some of our stupidest actions. It is also worth mentioning the fundamental error of attribution, which Ciccotti illustrates with an example that will be familiar to academics: the student who assumes that "when the teacher answers him curtly, it's because he's an asshole, and not because the question is stupid."

But that's not all. The book also includes contributions from many authors keen to cast light on our small daily approximations in terms of reasoning, which the psychologist Daniel Kahneman calls "heuristics." A few examples from the business world:

- authority bias, which consists of taking seriously advice or orders given by people who appear to have—because of their appearance or their attire, for example a well-tailored suit or a smart white blouse—knowledge or know-how that you yourself do not possess;
- the framing bias, defined here by Kahneman: if "you are given the choice between two planes: the first has a 97% chance of arriving safely, the second has a 3% chance of crashing. Spontaneously, you tend to choose the first one whereas the risks are equivalent for both flights. The wording thus modifies our judgement";
- the illusion of causality, also known as the illusory correlation, when one simultaneously observes the rise in river water levels while interest rates are falling and hastily draws conclusions about the causal links between the two phenomena;
- the halo effect, which explains many recruitment errors, when we assume that the presence of a certain talent makes the individual likely to have other talents. Someone who is capable of doing small things is, it is believed, also capable of doing big things, and vice versa. Of course, this is not always the case; and
- loss aversion, which explains the reluctance to make investments often demonstrated by boards of directors: we are more affected by the idea of losing money than by making money.

In economics, everything seems logical, but nothing makes sense. We are constantly under the influence of our psyches in our tactical and strategic choices, and economic objects appear to have a psychological dimension, too. Even economists seem to admit as much, with Kahneman's work in the field earned him a Nobel Prize in Economics in 2002.

It is worth remarking that the very unexpected success of this book, which attempts with humor and elegance to make us a little less blind to ourselves, means that it is soon to be translated into fifteen languages. Since bullshit is universal, it is also an inexhaustible subject of study: proof that it was needed, a second volume is in the works.

May this success prove Tobie Nathan wrong: in a short interview at the end of the book, the writer reminds us that "when you psychoanalyse idiots, they become evil, because they become aware of their inadequacies." It's something we've all had the opportunity to observe in our professional lives: "Idiots don't like people who aren't idiots."

Idiocy in Organizations

Maxime Rovère, *Que faire des cons? Pour ne pas en rester un soi-même*[14] (Paris: Flammarion, 2019).

Can we imagine a world, especially a professional one, without stupidity? Not if we believe the vision of the world presented by Mats Alvesson and André Spicer in *The Stupidity Paradox*, or the various authors who have since followed in their footsteps: Jean-François Marmion has given us a "psychology of stupidity," François Bégaudeau has offered up a "history of your stupidity," and Spinoza specialist Maxime Rovère has had considerable success with this essay in the form of an investigation. Whether we prefer to talk of stupidity or, more radically, idiocy, it seems that no organization can escape it and that the phenomenon is forever proliferating under the guise of complacency, cretinism, even cultism.

What Rovère describes is a cause of genuine concern for management: it would seem that no project can escape it, because those whom he joyfully calls "the idiots," of whom there is no shortage, appear to be in charge. There is no way to do without them unless, the author tells us, you are either God or dead. Nor is there any way to escape from the "stupidity of structures, constantly remaking and undoing society . . . by which it is shaped in return." You can't escape it, because this is precisely what defines the specific form of unintelligence identified by the author: a will to remain as you are without learning anything from what happens.

In trying to answer the question that gives the book its title, Rovère deploys three arguments that may come as a surprise.

The first is to remind readers that stupidity always involves "an emotional relationship," which is why it is so difficult to manage in our social lives. In the end, you can never completely avoid being blamed for the very thing you criticize in others. "In this sense, even if you hate the idea, you and the idiot are a team," he explains. Discerning stupidity in an interlocutor is like being part of a story in which, by blaming the victim, you run the risk of becoming a fool yourself. This is undoubtedly a timely manner of confronting our own limitations.

Second, if it is an emotional relationship, it means that we generally tend to cloak our reproaches in moral values. Addressing the idiot is always a bit like trying to lecture him. But, as our Spinozist says, nothing is worse than to try to reduce the gap between you and the person you think is a fool. Rovère turns educator when he advises that "instead of defending values, you would do better to develop relationships, in other words try to minimize misunderstandings."

Finally, he concludes with a shift of perspective, suggesting that stupidity is always ultimately an "event that occurs at the heart of human relationships, which cannot be ascribed to the types of humans walking around the world: this is the so-called interactional dimension of stupidity." He rightly notes that the rise of opportunities to communicate in society, through social media and other means, has constantly increased the possibilities for individuals to misunderstand one another, or at least to increase the opportunities for confusion and misunderstanding. Thus, jerks are no longer persons but simply "interactional entities."

Management could benefit from this analysis. Managers must understand that no one can abolish stupidity but everyone can contribute to its reduction by listening to those who suffer from it. It is a question of our ability to work together, always trying to limit our differences of interpretation, and keeping in mind that three strategies suggested by the author are finally possible: "negotiate with those who can, help those who want to develop to do so, and leave well alone those who refuse to change."

Creativity at Work

Gilles Amado, Jean-Philippe Bouilloud, Dominique Lhuilier, and Anne-Lise Ulmann (under the direction of), *La Créativité au travail*[15] (Érès, 2017).

Is "creativity at work" a fair aspiration of individuals, or rather an injunction from on high, especially from managerial discourse? If creativity is a legitimate expectation managers and employees in organizations share, is it not simply a concrete and daily response to the gap between managerial expectations and the desire we feel to be creative rather than repetitive? "Living creatively is always more important for the individual than doing well," as the American psychoanalyst Donald Winnicott reminds us.[16]

For the four authors of this book, creativity is first and foremost a concrete and daily response to the gap work as prescribed and the work done, between work as commissioned and work as experienced. It thus consists of a permanent adjustment, a constant adaptation to the obstacles encountered in the diverse circumstances of professional life. It can be both a day-to-day strategy to get around obstacles and an experience of play, inventiveness, practical intelligence, part of what Michel de Certeau called the "arts of doing." The sociologist Marie-Anne Dujarier notes, for example, that academic studies have shown "that workers collectively transformed their (difficult and absurd) task into a game, imbuing it with new meaning: it is no longer a question of moving metal plates but of beating speed scores, of taunting the foreman," in short, "of inventing competitions with colleagues, in whose company it is possible to demonstrate one's virtuosity."

All of that amounts to another way of saying that creativity is linked to the much broader question of meaning at work. This book is, therefore, situated at the crossroads of transversal approaches originating in work studies, clinical psychoanalysis, psychosociology, and educational sciences. It shows how creativity differs from innovation in the strict sense of the word: whereas the latter concerns a "process of influence in the service of change," as the editors put it, creativity "concerns the subject at work and, conversely, work in the subject."

Henceforth, two competing conceptions stand out clearly: that of the sociologist Danièle Linhard, who describes an atmosphere of subjective insecurity because managers, more or less consciously, are afraid of this creativity in that it enables employees to distinguish more clearly between their personal interests and the interests of the company. The opposing view is represented by Thomas Paris, a specialist in the creative industries, for whom, on the contrary, "creation appears to be one of the last refuges of subjectivity in a world which is becoming increasingly obsessed with rationality."

Faced with these two antinomic perspectives, the cartoon by René Pétillon (a recently deceased cartoonist well known to faithful readers of *Le Canard Enchaîné*), included at the end of the book alongside an intriguing interview of the cartoonist by the sociologist Jean-Philippe Bouilloud, provides a fitting conclusion. The cartoon shows an unpleasant-looking rock star instructing some poor bloke at a piano to "write me a hit." Creativity is not necessarily immune to tyranny. What is creative freedom? Is it the right to refuse to make a hit? Or to the contrary, should the songwriter be happy to simply serve up something in the mainstream format that the market demands?

Pétillon concludes by acknowledging that "the existence of satirical cartoons is a guarantee of democracy," of course, but that "the newspapers that publish them do not operate in a democratic way." A beautiful paradox, and food for thought for those among us who pride themselves on their organizational creativity.

Cretinization versus De-automation

Bernard Stiegler, L'emploi est mort vive le travail[17] **(Mille et une nuits, 2015).**

Do we know what kind of technical world we live in? Do we understand the workings of the systems, particularly the computer systems, that surround us and remotely control our daily actions, our decisions, our purchases, and probably, to a certain extent, our votes?

For the most part we don't, and we are unable to grasp its full complexity. In the space of a few microseconds, billions of bytes of data can be transmitted and processed with the help of algorithms, a quantity that is simply inconceivable to us. The machines themselves are the repositories of the knowledge entrusted to them; meanwhile, we pretend not to notice, even though our models of existence are already being radically altered by mass marketing and automation. Faced with the immense possibilities that intensive computing and the quantitative handling of data offer, we no longer possess any capacity to counter the anticipation of our every impulse by these predictive systems.

For the philosopher Bernard Stiegler, who sadly passed away in the summer of 2020, all the actors engaged in economic action are the willing victims of a phenomenon of proletarianization. By this word, he meant not an impoverishment but an erasure of knowledge, a progressive destruction of what we are capable of understanding, in favor of the computer systems that we use constantly. But these systems are becoming more and more intelligent as we, to an extent that we fail to recognize, continue to divest ourselves of all intrinsic knowledge. This amounts to cretinization, a term of endearment that Stiegler used liberally in relation to certain academic and political elites, and particularly to economic elites. He deployed it with particular vehemence in the case of Alan Greenspan, the former chair of the U.S. Federal Reserve, who admitted that he simply did not understand what was happening to the economy during the subprime crisis.[18]

How, exactly, does this trend represent a serious problem for the economy? Because it tends to impoverish the quality of each person's existence, as well as the quality of personal and collective work experience. So, what can be done about it? Stiegler's recommendation is to de-automatize our relationship to work, to rediscover the empowering potential of know-how, to put the emphasis on savoir-vivre, to put the sharing of knowledge back at the heart of human collaboration.

Finally, we must allow what cannot be standardized to regain the upper hand over what is already standardized. The author uses the example of a violinist to illustrate the fact that "to work is to implement a capacity for invention based on received automatisms, which is acquired when one is able to de-automatize them." A little later he adds:

> The virtuoso becomes an artist when he proves capable of inverting automatisms without foreknowledge, of making a fork, of interpreting beyond the automatisms specific to the instrument.

Interpretation and creation thus become possible, even desirable again.

This concise book, consisting mainly of an interview with the journalist Ariel Kyrou, develops important ideas from one of the few philosophers to have taken a close interest in economic issues, notably through the Ars Industrialis association.[19] It is an accessible introduction to an important body of thought sometimes considered difficult and will provide much-needed inspiration to those for whom culture is the basis of economic development. And not the other way around.

Should We Submit to the Ideology of Innovation?

Benoît Godin, *Innovation Contested. The Idea of Innovation over the Centuries* (Abingdon: Routledge, 2015).

Benoît Godin and Dominique Vinck, *Critical Studies in Innovation (Alternative Approaches to the Pro-Innovation Bias)* (Cheltenham: Elgar, 2017).

Whatever our position in an organization, we are required, or so it is believed, to innovate. And every one of us hopes one day to be described as an innovator, or at least not to be considered as opposed to innovation. Within organizations, we find two categories of individuals: those who innovate and those who do not. So, innovation has gradually become our sole criterion for evaluation. It is no longer a question of knowing whether an action is good or bad, but of determining whether it is sufficiently innovative, in which case it will be judged good; or not, in which case it must be considered bad. Innovation is associated with extraordinarily positive values, to the extent that it has become the keyword of the contemporary economy, the "superior strategy" of any organization of note in its market.

For Benoît Godin, a researcher at the INRS in Montreal, this whole business of innovation and the utopia it underpins is the result of a vast collective blindness. In the book he makes two key points.

First, the word innovation is itself in need of a more precise definition. Is innovation purely a matter of bringing something new to the table? Or can it be it the renewal of something old or unfashionable? Although the concept has acquired an incredible degree of influence in the present day, how does it relate to terms such as invention, favored for much of the nineteenth century, imagination, or even creation, the latter still preferred by artists? In becoming a catch-all term for the imaginative, creative, and inventive processes of organizations, has innovation lost its specific meaning?

Second, innovation has not always been regarded so positively: it was considered a negative force by the ancient Greeks, who saw it as a challenge to existing laws and morals and was regarded with only slightly less suspicion in the Middle Ages, when it was understood on a spiritual level: innovation then consisted of renewing one's soul. Today, it appears as the counterpoise to all organizational problems. Godin takes Machiavelli as an example: according to the Italian thinker, the world does not need innovation to change, because it changes all the time without anyone's help. This is why, if innovation has a role, it is first to help stabilize power, not to transform it, because circumstances and the principle of reality naturally take care of this. This is quite the opposite of what we imagine innovation to be, in the most banal sense: the world is moving, and organizations are too rigid; they must be pushed around so that they adapt, by innovating.

Developing a critical approach to innovation, therefore, seems to be the only way out of what can only be called an ideology. This is what Benoît Godin attempts to do, with the help of Dominique Vinck and the many contributors to this collective work. In it we find discussions of aspects that are often overlooked, such as resistance to innovation, imitation, or mimicry. We also encounter the idea that if managers like the term "innovation" so much, it is because they consider it to be the reason for whatever success they might achieve. The more innovative their vision, the more successful their company will be in the market. It is interesting to note, however, that when observing the difficulties of their competitors, their attitude is quite different: it is not their fault but due to negative external factors. Psychologists call this phenomenon attribution error: if I innovate and win, it's because of me; if others lose, it's because they were not lucky enough.

Contemplating the by-now familiar deluge of clichés surrounding the term, we can surely agree with the authors of these two titles: the time has come to critically distance ourselves from the ambiguous, equivocal concept of innovation.

Reinventing the Right to Laziness?

Tom Hodgkinson, *How to Be Idle* (New York: Harper Perennial, 2007).

"O silent murderer, Laziness, keep no more / My spirit imprisoned / And you, Sleep, do not leave me / Lose another hour in your society."[20] Describing her morning awakening in these terms, patrician poet Hannah More sought to remind her contemporaries of the dangers of nonchalance, of excessive repose, of any form of relaxation, basically.

Tom Hodgkinson, on the other hand, takes quite the opposite view: "After a good night . . . I feel like a different person," he confides. "I am cheerful, forgiving and helpful. I am also more efficient. I can do a day's work in three or four hours, leaving a lot more time for idling." Arriving late at the office is not a problem, far from it, as long as one arrives in tip-top form and not overwhelmed by fatigue. In support of this argument, he cites Karl Marx's son-in-law Paul Lafargue's *Right to Laziness*, which reminds us that "God himself, after working for six days, has rested for eternity."

In this short and, in places, joyous essay, the creator of the magazine *The Idler*, founded more than twenty-five years ago, sets out to reassert the value of slowness. He takes great delight in reminding us that, in the mid-nineteenth century, it was fashionable to walk a turtle rather than a dog in the most fashionable districts. He also mounts a valiant defense of napping, teatime, and fishing to fulfill John Maynard Keynes's assertion in his economic possibilities for our grandchildren that "the day will come when we will know how to honour those . . . delightful people who are capable of taking direct enjoyment in things, the lilies of the field who toil not, neither do they spin." Which also constitutes a robust riposte to Gordon Gekko, the antihero of Oliver Stone's *Wall Street*,[21] who proclaims, "Lunch is for wimps!"

For our cheerfully lazy essayist, nothing seems more important than a luncheon spent in enriching conversation, rather than chewing alone. He is a partisan of slow food, and a staunch opponent of the post-meal coffee, which he argues excites nervousness rather than efficiency, increases the dose of stress and the chances of developing an ulcer, nothing very beneficial, it must be admitted, for the lucidity we all need in professional life.

The author also pokes fun at sleep skeptics, borrowing the words of a character from a Jonathan Coe novel who says the following about a certain former British prime minister: "Can you imagine what it means for a woman of Margaret Thatcher's calibre, with her strength of character, to be forced to remain prostrate each night in this lamentable posture of submission? The brain out of control, the muscles flaccid and inert? It must be unbearable."

In fine, this plea for relaxation can be read as a defense of true availability. The lazy person must be prompt if he wants to be able to rest longer. The lazy person must also be entrepreneurial, in the sense of Mark Twain's character

Tom Sawyer, "using his ingenuity to convince others to do the thankless work while he watches horse races from his private box on a Tuesday afternoon."

However, this definition does not correspond to the figure of the adventurous entrepreneur,[22] as developed by Vladimir Jankélévitch, who sees the adventure itself as its own purpose. On the other hand, this paean to the pleasures of taking one's time has the merit of bringing us back to the classic distinction between otium, the time of contemplation and leisure, and negotium, the activity of trade. The Stoic philosophers were not mistaken on this count; in their view, it was important to keep both. The maintenance of otium, which is priceless, mixed with negotium, which ensures the subsistence of each, was in Seneca's eyes the essential alliance for the life of the wise man. With, of course, an important caveat addressed to the idle man: "Virtue placed in leisure without action is but an incomplete and feeble thing, because he never displays what he has learned."

The Art of Putting It Off until Tomorrow

John Perry, *The Art of Procrastination: A Guide to Effective Dawdling, Lollygagging and Postponing* (Workman Publishing, 2012).

Acrasy, or "delicacy of will," is a notion that management research really should study more closely. All too often, good strategic visions, although supported by very good communication, have little impact because managers fail at the moment of "doing," at the moment of implementing their wishes, due to a lack of determination. Or they do act but in a way that contradicts to their own promises and expectations.

Before becoming a management issue, acrasy (akrasia) was a problem for the ancient Greeks, as the philosopher John Perry, professor emeritus at Stanford University, points out. Procrastination is the art, or affliction, if you prefer, of always putting off until tomorrow what one could do today. Procrastinators are always late with their promises, while paradoxically being ahead of schedule on matters that are not urgent. In this respect, procrastinators are impervious to deadlines since they take them at face value: they are "dead lines," or dead ends.

The phenomenon is not particularly rare, we might by reassured to learn—there is even a world day, March 25, dedicated to procrastination. The initiators of this operation explain that it is "an opportunity for the followers of this attitude to take a break to reflect on the constraints of the modern world, as well as the frantic pace of life it imposes."

Indeed, this involuntary postponement of daily life can have very harmful consequences for those who are inclined to it, as the letters received by Perry show. This inclination may simply distract individuals from having constructive relationships with others, as well as with themselves, so much so that they are powerless to avoid letting themselves down.

In these pages, Perry invites us to think differently about the impact of permanent reprogramming, of procrastination as a source of guilt—self-administered, moreover. He develops the idea that it is important to be a structured procrastinator. He urges us, for example, to learn to sort out our imperatives, following the model of emergency doctors, and not to hesitate to break down the major tasks that fall to us into successive small tasks, which Perry suggests we list for ourselves. From then on, we should not hesitate to congratulate ourselves on ticking off tasks as we go along, even if this involves a certain degree of self-deception to encourage us to go all the way. In this way, we need not contemplate the immensity or the urgency of the achievement considered as a whole. Structured procrastinators are efficient people, argues the author, because they are first and foremost horizontal organizers who give free rein to their curiosity without getting too attached to time chains.

It should be noted, however, that on his website *structuredproscrastina tion.com*, the initiator of this amusing concept (although perhaps more serious than it appears at first glance) does not free us from commitments made in the past. But he does allow us to put certain ideas back into their right place regarding emergency management; despite the popular adage, procrastination sometimes proves to be a triple necessity: because we must think before acting, because some things can wait, and because others will sort themselves out.

Indeed, the latter point appears to be a fine example of practical wisdom. Or, as Perry puts it, let us "never do anything today that can disappear by tomorrow."

Can Managers' Dreams Be Interpreted?

Bernard Lahire, *The Sociological Interpretation of Dreams* (Polity Press, 2020).

A recent advertisement posted in the Paris metro was titled "Enter as a dreamer, leave as a manager." The ad in question was for a management school and seemed to imply that "dreaming" is one of two key requirements for "becoming a manager." The other, apparently, was to enroll at this school. To make our dreams come true, we thus need to know how to manage, but to make that possible, we first must dream. To become a good manager, let's start by dreaming.

In reality, this poster is an extension of what we believe we do when we dream. Dreams have long been viewed as potentially prophetic, an idea embodied by ancient "oneirokrites" (interpreters of dreams) such as

Artemidorus Daldianus, writing in the second century AD, who saw dreams as a kind of inspiration from the heavens. Or else, and this is the most widely shared contemporary understanding, dreams are believed to reflect the unconscious set of our unsatisfied desires, expressed during sleep time. This is the heart of the psychoanalytical approach: the dream emits frustrations, or aspirations, which are related to the Oedipus complex, guilt, and so on.

With this important book, Bernard Lahire completely turns on its head the understanding of and approach to dreams that have prevailed since Freud. According to this sociologist, professor at the Ecole Normale Supérieure in Lyon, our dreams are, first, trapped in the vice of our social life. To put it simply: management students dream of companies more often than those who study drawing, who are more likely to dream of masterpieces than those who learn music. In other words, dreams are not "distributed" randomly but depend on our social environment, our personal and professional life paths. "Brothers and sisters of disabled people dream about the problematic situation of disability," explains Lahire. "As for children living in combat zones, they dream of war scenes."

Despite the credit he gives to Sigmund Freud throughout the informed discussion that forms the framework of the book, Lahire criticizes his approach to dream materials. In the manner of liberal economists reducing the motivations of the economic actor to the maximization of self-interest, the great psychoanalyst and his followers tended to focus too much on the sexual and unconscious interpretation of dreams to the detriment of a more ingrained understanding of their social character. For Bernard Lahire, however, dreams are not a place of repression but, he argues, of "self-communication" and the most "intimate of our diaries" because they occur "without an external audience."

Contrary to the idea that dreams are projections of our hopes or our frustrations, they are first and foremost spaces in which the problems of our existence are posed, where our fears are expressed, and where the means to get out of these situations may be found. This is why the studies cited highlight that it is not often pleasant situations that are at the heart of our dreams but, rather, the difficulties we encounter, especially at work: job interviews, annual appraisal interviews, and requests for pay raises are all frequently reported dream scenarios. Ultimately, the dreamer reaffirms her anxieties, tries to thwart the necessities of reality in an attempt to see more clearly, in a language that belongs to her alone—extending the distant intuition of Heraclitus, who wrote that "those who are awake are in the same world," certainly, "but those who sleep are in a particular world."

So, dreams are perhaps not very magical after all. They are an expression of the self like any other, like public speeches, the narration of our fantasies or words spoken under hypnosis. So, how can we learn how to decipher what is in our dreams ourselves? Unfortunately, it is in the second volume, still awaiting publication, that the methodology of interpretation proposed by the author will be further established. Perhaps one day, a new way of understanding our dreams will be revealed to us, unraveling our inner conflicts to better live with our emotions. Managers and executives can always dream of this.

Teaching Poetry to Managers

Jean-Louis Chrétien, *Fragilité*[23] (Editions de Minuit, 2017).

VUCA: this somewhat simplistic acronym, sometimes used in management to describe the state of the world, at least has the merit of underlining the fact that decision makers often struggle to understand the environment in which they find themselves. Volatility, uncertainty, complexity, and ambiguity, four notions of a different and incomparable nature, nevertheless agree on one thing: the vulnerability of managers—as well as of our societies in general, as the health crisis of 2020 has shown—is beyond doubt.

For a philosopher such as Paul Ricoeur, recognizing the vulnerability of decision makers within organizations, whether they are company directors or surgeons, represents an opportunity for them to better exercise their capacities, but also to better glimpse their shortcomings (and therefore potentially to fill in any gaps). It is as if making a decision with an uncertain outcome is like experiencing one's own responsibility in a situation where one's own responsibility is at stake.

But can the same be said of fragility? In his latest essay, the philosopher and poet Jean-Louis Chrétien makes a clear distinction between the two notions:

> Vulnerable is that which can be injured, which implies an attack from outside. Only the living, in the broadest sense of the word, since it can be said of a tree, is susceptible to injury, whereas "fragile" can be used to describe inanimate beings.

Following, in particular, the paths traced out by the Fathers of the Church, Chrétien shows that deep down this fragility is constitutive, that it is never completely avoidable. The efforts of the Stoic philosophers in this direction appear to be insignificant and ultimately ineffective against our native fragility. As the author expresses it, "in his description of human frailty, St. Ambrose frequently uses the adjective lubricus in the general sense of 'slippery,' and therefore unstable, uncertain, perilous."

But to all this we could answer that, contrary to what he suggests, the exact antonym has existed since 2012, when Nassim Nicholas Taleb published his book *Antifragile*. In a linguistic contortion worthy of *1984*'s "newspeak," this essayist hastily decreed that the exact antonym of fragile was antifragile. An antifragile would be that which becomes stronger after an aggression, after a pile-up. With the concept of antifragile, we move beyond resistance and resilience into a realm of extreme mithridatism, where each car crash becomes a boon, each accident an opportunity, each poison absorbed by mistake a beneficial hazard.

Faced with this improbable fiction, Jean-Louis Chrétien's book seems a good if not foolproof antidote, at least to the temptation of mistaking bladders for lanterns, of mistaking for indestructible and divine things that appear unbreakable and in reality are fragile.

If Ricoeurian vulnerability brings us back to responsibility, the recognition of our fragility confronts us with the sometimes "slippery" nature of the ambiguous and uncertain situations experienced in organizations. Some management researchers have suggested that we do not need skills per se but "negative capabilities" (Keats). According to him, these qualities are those encountered "when a man is capable of being in uncertainties, mysteries, doubts, without any irritable reaching after fact and reason."

Basically, they allow us to measure ourselves fearlessly against our difficulties, our limits, sometimes our worries, to better surpass them when the opportunity presents itself, if that opportunity ever presents itself. Has the time finally come to teach poetry to managers?

What We Talk about When We Talk about Leadership

Within management's pantheon of taboo terms, leadership is certainly one of the most recurring and important concepts. It is presented as a tacit theory of organizations, as an oversimplification that can explain the precise reason for the success or failure of any project, any company, any team. Starting from the symbolic, even mythical, character of the main leader or leader, it seeks to explain the whole organization.

Moreover, leadership research has always distinguished between two possible approaches to the notion: either the leader is guided by a personal ambition, she is the guide, or even the "raison d'être of the organization,"[24] or else she embodies a collective ambition, a common purpose, of which she may be considered an incarnation. More recently, much of the literature on these issues has leaned toward the latter option, taking up notions such as shared leadership[25] or relational leadership,[26] which acknowledge a transformation in the relationship to hierarchical power and the classic forms of leadership that new generations are said to be demanding. The phenomena of reverse monitoring, the disappearance of the monopoly on expertise held by the most experienced employees, are indeed very important factors of transformation.

It is to seek further insights into these questions that the works reviewed here should be examined. They begin by asking us about the conditions in which power is exercised in open societies, as well as the competition from machines, which may soon exercise it in our place. But they also reexamine the qualities of the leader, whether functional or charismatic, of the one who "takes" power (Lignier), from European (Tavoillot) or American (Pfeffer) perspectives. We can see that these questions, which are, incidentally, quite theoretical, find an echo in a certain number of the fictional "great narratives" of our time. Questions illustrated, for example, by the TV show *House of Cards*, which brilliantly explores the difference between a "good leader" and a "good person as leader." Such issues have been addressed in broader terms in the wildly successful *Game of Thrones*, based on the novels by G. R. R. Martin, which continually reexamines the question of whether we need a leader.

Reality and fiction are thus intertwined in a new cartography of power, prompting Nassim Nicholas Taleb to propose that we question the asymmetries that exist within organizational life, arguing that only those with "skin in the game" truly deserve to be listened to.

But perhaps it is to new forms of "entrepreneurial adventure" that we should be looking for the emergence of a renewed and rejuvenated relationship to power. Although, of course, this should not prevent us from regarding with a certain scepticism the utopian claims made for self-entrepreneurship, as well as Alain Deneault's thesis on the emergence of a "mediocracy,"[27] the fruit of the encounter between the impoverishment of language and a principle of "normalcy," the bias of those who choose the system without ever questioning it. Against "mediocrats," therefore, depressed incarnations of power in organizations, perhaps we should, on the contrary, reaffirm the power of disobedience, or even the force of "no," as indirectly suggested by authors (such as Frédéric Gros and Vincent Delecroix) who have devoted essays[28] to contemporary forms of insubordination. Two possible horizons hover into view: the complete disappearance of any form of authority favored by social media, what Umberto Eco called "the invasion of the fools" or, more promisingly, the return to forms of "leader/follower" relationships, which I will discuss later in this book as well, capable of yielding discrete, almost invisible successes, helping to reconcile us to the benefits of collaborative work.

Finally, the progress of neurobiology, which Antonio Damasio discusses, opens up an interesting perspective in two ways: on the one hand, by demonstrating that the search for new forms of governance adapted to what he calls "the strange order of things" cannot be dissociated from biological and scientific questions. On the other hand, by showing that questions of organization, science and even culture ("Life, feelings and the making of culture," as the subtitle of the book would have it) can hardly be dissociated, a subject explored by other authors discussed hereunder.

Horizontality and Verticality in Management

Niall Ferguson, *The Square and the Tower: Networks and Power, from the Freemasons to Facebook* (New York: Penguin, 2017).

Imagine yourself in the Piazza del Campo in Siena, Italy, where the Palio, a horse race in which the city's districts compete against each other, is held every year. In this seashell-shaped square, one of the most magical places in Europe, what do you see? Opposite, the majestic Torre del Mangia, towering over the cathedral, all the better to signify the equivalence of secular and religious powers. All around, the market square is transformed into a racecourse when necessary, but above all it offers a space where the crowds of people trade, exchange, conduct transactions, "do business," as we say today.

In his latest work, British historian Niall Ferguson revisits the history of the great transformations of the Western world, the Reformation, the Enlightenment, and the scientific revolution, based on this image of force divided between two distinct poles: old hierarchies on the one hand, disruptive networks on the other. On the one hand, the emerging face of power, which is visible and can also be frightening, which believes it has a monopoly on authority. On the other hand, its immersed side, multiple networks, commercial, militant, educational, or terrorist, which, to use a Dickensian expression employed by the author, "are situated upstream and downstream of the river" and above all operate based on more or less unofficial affinities, interests, and links. It is these two organizational forces that, according to Ferguson, make up history—History with a capital H.

This argument is congruent with the results of management research on at least three decisive points:

- the confirmed presence, beyond the official organization chart, of an informal organization: "When a boss is accused by some employees of favouritism," explains Ferguson, "the implication is that some informal relationships are taking precedence over the formal promotion process. . . . When employees from different firms meet for alcoholic refreshments after work, they move from the vertical tower of the corporation to the horizontal place of the social network";
- the importance for any individual leader of strengthening their "personal coalition." In a well-executed passage focusing on the example of Henry Kissinger, the former U.S. secretary of state, Ferguson shows how

Kissinger spent his life maintaining personal and intellectual links with all kinds of interlocutors, sometimes enemies of America; and

- last, a growing concern among management researchers, the importance of networks in the success of any company, to the point that hierarchies themselves have their own. Within the scientific community in management studies, many are now observing that the functioning of social networks, independent and flexible, is more important for the transformation of companies than political life itself.

But our historian distinguishes himself here precisely by trying to find a middle way, beware of any naive veneration for horizontal power systems, while firmly rejecting conspiracy theories—even as he highlights the role of the Illuminati, who did indeed exist in Germany at the end of the eighteenth century, in the processes leading up to the French Revolution. Yet it is precisely because it was minor that their role is recognized today, because the more we hear about a network, the less effective it has been. A network's notoriety is inversely proportional to its real power, which consists only in shaking up hierarchies.

To sum up, let us ask the question the author himself posed: "Is it better today to be in a network, which gives influence, or in a hierarchy, which gives power?" In reality, the formal and the informal, the visible and the invisible, the vertical and the horizontal always coexist. When trust is not total in a society, hierarchies are necessary. When networks of influence take all the power, then the interests of a few take precedence over the common good.

To paraphrase another master of political philosophy—namely, Blaise Pascal—we could say that "the square needs the tower to apply itself, the tower needs the square to legitimise itself. The square without a tower is contradicted, because there will always be bad guys. The tower without the square is accused. So the tower and the square must exist together."

On Government and Consent

Pierre-Henri Tavoillot, *Comment gouverner un peuple roi? Traité nouveau d'art politique*[29] (Odile Jacob, 2019).

During the 1992 American election that pitted George H. W. Bush against Bill Clinton, "only 15 percent of voters knew that the candidates were in favor of the death penalty, but 86 percent knew the name of George Bush's dog." By reminding us of this brief anecdote, the philosopher Pierre-Henri Tavoillot appears to offer a disturbing critique of the liberal democratic system, a system that he nevertheless proposes by means of a passionate reinvention.

He has no doubt at all about the difficulties that the liberal system constantly throws up, mentioned by Georges Clémenceau in this famous aphorism: "To reach a decision you need an odd number of people, and three is already too many." This quotation seems never to have been so topical. It increasingly seems that the liberal democratic model, on all continents of the globe, is faltering every day in the face of illiberal alternatives such as the Singapore model, theocentric alternatives such as in Turkey, or radical alternatives, as proposed by many revolutionary parties. And, lest we forget, even France is prey to a widespread sense of ill-focused rage against those in power, spectacularly embodied by the Yellow Vests movement, which came as a shock to both the government and traditional intermediary bodies.

What political art is capable of rehabilitating the consent to be governed, the pillar of any democratic project? Are we still capable of reconciling democracy and efficiency? asks the author, as if to remind us that in a democracy, it is certainly the people who decide, but the people, as Proudhon said, "are hardly democrats since they generally only aspire to confide in the first dictator who comes along."

The people, moreover, is a concept that is polysemic, to say the least. One may adopt a narrow definition of the concept: the people is, then, the whole of the members of a nation subjected to the same laws. But we can also adopt a broader vision: is the people the totality of voters, half of the votes plus one, or the voice of those who know how to make themselves heard better than others? Moreover, as Tavoillot notes, Robespierre after 1789, Stalin after 1924, and Hugo Chavez in 2012 all felt moved to exclaim, "I am the people!"

Ultimately, whatever one's conception of it, the notion of peoplehood requires a political art, and it is the whole point of this book to suggest one. This political art, which Tavoillot describes in outline form, is defined on the basis of four highly disparate aspects: first, knowing how to convince to win elections; then, being able to enter into a discussion process to draw up a concrete program of action; then, knowing how to decide as an arbitrator; and finally, submitting (this is the role of intermediate elections) to the popular judgment that can be read in the results obtained.

Two remarks spring to mind. First, it should be noted that these four missions are perfectly heterogeneous, each understanding that the qualities of a boatman during an election campaign have nothing to do with those of an accountant who submits his copy to his leader Next, it is striking just how much the political art presented by Tavoillot has in common with the art of management. Both are founded upon a feedback loop that goes from appointment to reporting and back again, in a cycle of permanent learning. Nothing is "natural" about these arts, and they demand qualities that are ultimately contradictory: being ambitious and measured, benevolent and decisive, confident and doubtful all at the same time.

In the end, our democracy is based on a strange wager, a wager that the author mischievously calls "the extension of the adult domain." On the one hand, a citizen capable of "obeying": Tavoillot reminds us that "in the etymological sense (ob-audire)," obeying means "to lend an ear," not "to give one's will." On the other hand, leaders of the city who are not only functional managers, as they are more and more frequently, but leaders capable of adding grace, charisma, that "je-ne-sais-quoi-presque-tout" that impresses us so much when it is present and "remains an enigma when it has disappeared." Just like Xenophon's description of Cyrus, who managed at the same time to be "a good son, an older brother, a strict but fair father, an attentive mother and a sublime lover."

The Damage of the Vulgar

Bertrand Buffon, Vulgarité et Modernité[30] (Gallimard, Le Débat, 2019).

Bertrand Buffon pulls no punches in his remarks on certain actresses appearing at the Cannes Film Festival:

> They ostensibly claim to be elegant when everything in their appearance and attitude betrays their ignorance of the subject—unseemly, flashy clothes, the desire to tease rather than please, borrowed poses, a graceless look: they don't distinguish themselves, they simply make themselves noticed.

This essay bemoans the continuous extension of the territories of bad taste and general mediocrity in the political, economic, and artistic spheres.

Vulgarity has two very distinct meanings: it is certainly synonymous with impropriety, even coarseness, which particularly affects individuals who believe they are immune to it. Vulgarity is never more obvious than when it ignores itself and when those who ignore their own vulgarity are content to be as they are. Then one comes close to "shamelessness, exhibitionism, the delivery of one's soul, one's body, one's intimacy, without reserve, with disconcerting and embarrassing complacency": precisely the same problem faced by Molière's *Bourgeois Gentilhomme*, in fact.

But another meaning of the word considers as vulgar everything that is banal, down-to-earth; in fact, everything that comes from the people. This is the original meaning, developed by Mme de Staël in 1802, of a shame that settles down in front of the vulgus, the man in the street, the unremarkable, the trivial who participates in the crowd—that is to say, for the Swiss-born novelist, the revolutionaries of the Third Estate. In short, the author notes, "democracy and vulgarity happen simultaneously." Provided one is a democrat, this second orientation naturally raises many questions, particularly at a time when these different forms of vulgarity are expressed more than ever, in the street, on television sets, or on the Web. But everything is being relaunched in a new way today, insofar as the elites themselves are the prime instigators.

Drawing upon a whole gallery of examples provided by politicians, even elected ones, who are not distinguished either by their refinement or by their general culture, Buffon shows that vulgarity is no longer the prerogative of the lower class, as in the eighteenth century, or of the bourgeoisie, as in the nineteenth century, but has become established at the highest level of many states, with a whole range of nuances, because vulgarity can be intellectual or factual, bland or ostensible, debonair or bellicose—the worst form.

To understand this degradation, no explanation is more plausible than that of the oblivion of, or contempt for, the liberal arts in educational projects aimed at training future decision makers. To evoke this lack of taste and sensitivity for beautiful things, the Greeks had a word, apeirokalia, which Leo Strauss translated precisely as "vulgarity." Without education in ethics and aesthetics, so-called leaders find themselves powerless in the face of vulgarity in the performance of their duties, even calling for help.

So, how can we resist the rise of so much vulgarity? Let us once again put our trust in women, for it is they who throughout history have borne the brunt of the battle against coarseness, as illustrated here by several examples, including that of the writer Lydie Salvayre who, in her *Portrait of the Writer as a Domesticated Animal*, argues that "the times are considered 'vulgar' on the grounds, among other things, that tact is now considered a weakness," that "erudition is considered a pretension, self-effacement an infirmity and manners an obstacle to enjoyment."

This Delicate Art of Taking

Wilfried Lignier, *Prendre. Naissance d'une pratique sociale élémentaire*[31] (Seuil: Liber, 2019).

Can we look at consumer behavior or homo oeconomicus without looking at early childhood, and more specifically at the way in which young children acquire the ability to access objects?

It is generally accepted in microeconomics that it is not important to study very young children as they are not yet fully socialized. Received wisdom holds that only once they have left crèche do children become objects of social study, the idea being that this first experience of life in a collective environment serves to socialize them. A gesture as elementary as taking an object could therefore only be understood after this period of life, when society and its system of constraints has finally imposed its rights.

This is not, however, the point of view of the sociologist Wilfried Lignier, a specialist in childhood aligned with the sociogenesis of practices, who defends the idea that, whatever economists and psychologists might think, children do not become social from a very young age . . . because they are social from the outset. The place where the parents live, the family's eating habits, the number of siblings, to name but a few factors, all influence the way in which children perceive the world around them. So much so that the simple act of taking, generally conceived as a natural, impulsive act, depends on it.

The book plunges us into the universe of a Parisian crèche for children ages two to three, where the author observes the first gripping gestures that the children exercised. How does a child start to desire this or that object? How does he make himself understood by others, especially when they seem to have the same desire to "take"? Do boys and girls act in the same way? Do socially disadvantaged or advantaged children react differently in controlling things in their environment?

The experiment yielded more than its fair share of surprises. First, it very rapidly emerges, far from the clichés about pure child innocence, that a certain violence is part of children's lives. The role of the child-care assistants is often to try to contain this violence. In particular, it is apparent that "taking is a more elementary practice than giving," which prompts the observation that "the child 'consumer' precedes the child 'distributor'—logically and temporally." The authors also suggest that the relationship to property among working-class children is not the same: for them, owning is a matter of holding something in one's hand, whereas claiming ownership of a book, for example, is a gesture more usually made by children of higher social origin.

Finally, Lignier notes a particularly striking element: "at the crèche, desire depends on the desire of others. I have several times observed scenes where a child began to covet a certain object precisely because one or more other children were trying to take it." The more an object is the object of someone else's desire, the more valuable it becomes. So it is with children themselves: the more they value themselves, the more they become those with whom others want to be connected. One can read in these behaviors a flagrant return of the girardian theory of mimetic desire: desire is always imitation of the desire of others, and rivalry between beings finds its main source in it.

This study plunges us into a world that is no stranger to that of business organizations, where "taking" is an everyday act. Risks, markets, or options are constantly being taken. Sometimes we even take the bull by the horns, or our lives in our hands. In these operations, the manager undoubtedly plays a central role: it is up to her to define how and when to act. But how could she imagine being able to free herself from the bad habits acquired in early childhood? The study itself leaves us with some hope in this area, describing as "frustrating" the way children control their desires. It is the whole point of management education to encourage this development as much as possible.

Reclaiming Power over Machines?

Pascal Picq, *Qui va prendre le pouvoir? Les grands singes, les hommes politiques ou les robots*[32] (Paris: Odile Jacob, 2017)

What's the point of thinking if the machines can do it much more efficiently on our behalf? With the advent of artificial intelligence, especially conversational AI, we are entering a period in which machines will think more and more powerfully in our place. As a result, it will become less useful to think, so the reasoning goes, to the extent that this occupation will effectively be "outsourced" to our machines. This troubling scenario is evoked with considerable verve in the latest book from paleoanthropologist Pascal Picq, a great specialist in gorillas and other primates. In Picq's view, in this new, Darwinian digital space we have entered, human beings will only retain power if they succeed in facing up to two challenges simultaneously.

The first is to better understand the forms of natural intelligence that preceded ours, especially those of the great apes, of which he paints a fascinating portrait in the first chapters. Picq has no equal when it comes, for example, to the fascinating parallels between the alliance strategies used by vervets or baboons to gain power against the dominant males, and the concrete difficulties encountered by several of our politicians, particularly French ones.

The second effort to avoid becoming slaves to robots, which have become our new masters, would require the human species to refuse to give ground in terms of its muscular or neuronal dynamism. In other words, these new forms of intelligence should encourage us to always use the one we know we are capable of. They should even encourage us to push back our own limits.

This reasoning finds an echo in fiction. For Picq, in fact, this situation is similar to that described in 1963 by the author of *Planet of the Apes*, Pierre Boulle, through the testimony of this woman imprisoned in the jails of the chimpanzees who took power, and who explains that this situation was made possible by the inactivity of humans, by their refusal to make the slightest effort, by their apathy, making them slip little by little into a state of voluntary slavery. This is the degradation that awaits us if we do not take Darwin's lesson into account, warns this lecturer at the Collège de France: "Understanding what has made us successful is not enough to adapt to the world we have helped to change."

In passing, Pascal Picq offers scathing assessments of two familiar totems: the first is the idea of a universal basic income, a concept so innovative that it appears in Thomas More's *Utopia*, published in the mid-sixteenth century. The second is Taylorism, the organization of work on a "linear, serial and cumulative" model, which he criticizes ruthlessly. Because adapting to the world we have helped to change will force us to learn to unlearn, to go through periods of activity and inactivity, to take a step back from what has happened, to regain creativity and a sense of responsibility.

Let us therefore rediscover our ability to say no to the machines, or else they will soon be the ones in charge, to our detriment.

Dominance and Arrogance: The Truth about Leadership

Jeffrey Pfeffer, *Leadership BS* (New York: HarperCollins, 2015).

Have you ever participated in a leadership seminar? For Jeffrey Pfeffer, professor at Stanford University, it doesn't matter whether your answer is positive or negative because these courses are useless. The proof is that what he calls "the leadership industry" continues to do very well, while leaders are still as bad and dissatisfied with themselves as ever.

The reason for all this? For Pfeffer, there is no doubt that these seminars deliver a series of lies: they incite participants to be modest, authentic, cooperative, to generate trust, whereas unfortunately one must face the facts: real leaders do exactly the opposite of all that. No, big companies are not run by humble, altruistic people, and unremarkable sorts are unlikely to be selected for an important job. Hence, explains Pfeffer, the role of marketing in making a career to make yourself better known: to obtain a better social status and greater influence, it is necessary not just to have self-confidence but to be even "overconfident"—(i.e., very self-confident). And that's not all: you still need energy to spare, charisma, and a certain spirit of superiority, as demonstrated by his synthetic overview of 187 studies devoted to this question.

In short, leadership teachers who try to inspire their learners are on the wrong track. They fail to take into account the tension that always exists within a social group between individual interests and maximizing the well-being of the group. In real life, Pfeffer assures us that leaders "eat first" (i.e., they always serve themselves first, contrary to the fantasy prescriptions of "servant leadership" that have developed here and there). Leaders have an unquenchable thirst to dominate, because the enjoyment of power is the rule. And Pfeffer quotes to illustrate all this the Homeric angers of Larry Ellison, Oracle CEO , and his approach to management based on the medieval rules used in their time by the samurai.

If Pfeffer's intention was to ridicule the American managerial system, it is hard to imagine a better approach. Admittedly, the desire for domination inspires many leaders—who would dare argue otherwise? That sometimes the so-called leaders also do the opposite of what they claim to do, often out of weakness of will, moreover, or akrasia, as the ancient Greeks said, who could disagree? Blaise Pascal already claimed this in his time when he wrote that "speeches of humility are a matter of pride to glorious people." Yet, as Pascal adds, “Few talk humbly of humility, few chastely of chastity, few doubtfully about doubt.” But visibly unable to make a clear distinction between a judgment of fact and a judgment of value, our author, as a distraught admirer of Ayn Rand’s theses on the passion of rational selfishness, functions as if the ethical aspect did not matter. Honesty about oneself, concern for others, and generosity in leading are bullshit, Pfeffer tells us.

To this we could be tempted to reply that never before have young graduates been so in search of meaning, as all recent surveys show, and that the desire to collaborate is so fundamental that, to use an image proposed by Yuval Noah Harari, it has enabled humans to visit the moon while chimpanzees devote themselves to throwing stones in zoos. Future leaders can only take this into account. As the Dane Sören Kierkegaard rightly pointed out in a short note:

> It is only when you are clever enough to want to build a system without introducing ethics that everything works well, that you have a system where you have everything, everything else, and where you have left out the only thing that is necessary.[33]

House of Cards's Lessons on Power

Emmanuel Taïeb, *House of Cards*. Le crime en politique[34] (PUF, 2018).

“The Americans don’t know what they need. I do. I know what they need.” Words spoken not by Donald Trump, but by Francis “Frank” Underwood, the Democratic majority leader, the chief whip who, in the TV show *House of Cards*, sets out to exact vengeance upon those who promised him a prominent place in government and failed to deliver. For Emmanuel Taïeb, a professor of political science, *House of Cards* depicts a Machiavellian universe where “only the triumph of a few counts, and where the destruction of others is a possible option.” The show can make one think of a “fictional refuge” in an America now prone to “Trumpism.”

But another possible reading emerges, because we might also regard this highly successful series as a long, very precise definition of leadership according to the precepts that Underwood describes facing the camera. For him, leadership is a combat sport: his conception of the exercise of power is guided by an absolute principle of individual success, access to and retention of power. A principle of individual success illustrated when we find Francis praying in church and telling us, “I pray for myself.” The principle of staying in power, meanwhile, ensures that Francis does not hesitate to get rid of journalists or competitors who might question his ascension to the supreme mandate. For Francis, a collaborator is always an asset, a resource, which only makes sense if he or she can be useful to him. "Do I believe in him?" "That's beside the point" is his answer. However high the potential there is, it should not be put at the service of any "ethics of discussion" but of a vertical management embodied just as well by his wife, Claire (with whom he forms a fusional and troubling couple) when she addresses one of his employees: "I run the organization. You work for her." Subordination has no limits.

In France, a coach wrote for a management magazine twenty-three life lessons based on the methods of the hero of this show. This little guide, which is still available online, allows you to understand, for example, the benefits of getting closer to power because, as Underwood points out:

> Power is a lot like real estate. It's all about location, location, location. The closer you are to the source, the higher your property value.

Managers are therefore advised to sit as close as possible to the boss in a meeting. But also not to whet the sharks' appetite, never justify your own actions, surround yourself with second knives, throw out false compliments before striking quickly and hard. And it is here that we must favor Taïeb's analysis, which confronts us, the spectators of the show, with our ambiguities as voters, because this is the singular transgression of the program: what exactly do we want when we elect an individual, for her to be good or to be effective? Underwood's expeditious methods are proving to be devilishly effective. Here's someone who can be described as "competent," with everything going on as if the show finally proved him right: "The Americans don't know what they need." But he does. He knows what they need. And the price to pay is the brutality of his authoritarianism.

Ultimately, the show does not offer a manual of good conduct; it sets out to dissect, for the ambivalent pleasure of the spectator, the risks of a leadership powered by pure ambition. Certainly, the permanence of self-esteem and the libido dominandi, the will to dominate, are at the very heart of any exercise of power, as many classical authors have noted, but the question that remains unanswered here is that of the leader's hubris, which no longer exercises authority over himself. With Underwood, the title of whip is fitting: it was originally applied to the valet, on horseback, who guided the hounds during a hunting expedition.

The Game of Thrones

"Games of Thrones," *Philosophie Magazine* (special issue, 2019).

On pain of being excluded from most dinner party conversations in the city, or even in the country, no one can claim to be unaware of the existence of

Game of Thrones, the medieval fantasy show that fascinated a considerable number of fans for eight years. Eight seasons made up of conquests, epics, and incessant betrayals, in a secular world imagined by an author from the American counterculture, George R. R. Martin. A world dominated by the sole balance of power, where no one ever thinks of turning the other cheek.

This series has generated a great deal of interest from management authors, resulting in the publication of all sorts of books, such as *Win or Die: Leadership Secrets from Game of Thrones* by Bruce Craven, or Winter is not coming: managers, dare to be entrepreneurial! There is no real reason to be surprised. In these books, we are told how the misadventures of one another are like lessons in political survival for the most ambitious of viewers: men being weak but treacherous; one must constantly learn to be wary of them. The book *Strategies of the Seven Kingdoms Applied to Working Life*, for example, shows what Tywin Lannister has in common with Steve Jobs, and underlines the importance of the network and personal coalition in power struggles. Just look at Littlefinger's social rise.

In reality, the series constantly confronts us with two managerial questions. The first one concerns family management. The story finally tells the story of the internal struggles within the great noble lineages (the Tyrells, the Martells, the Greyjoys) who are supposed to rule the world but are confronted with environmental and migratory dangers beyond their control. Subjected to their ancestral beliefs, such as supposing that a wall could prevent the migratory phenomenon, they have interests to protect but not great causes to defend. The hour calls for a higher view, where their immediate and unique objective remains to take a piece of power and preserve it at all costs.

A second question follows: in an organization, is there still a need for a leader? And if so, what are the reasons that lead to power, what is ultimately the motivation of the leader, and why would he or she be appointed?[35]

Through a chain of references to Plato or Hobbes, for example, the authors pose the central question of politics and leadership: who dominates, who is dominated, and why? This is the first reference to Plato, for whom accession to power presupposes not wanting it. In contrast to the case of the dreadful Joffrey Lannister, to whom his uncle Tywin reiterated in season 3 that "any man who has to say 'I am king' is not a real king." Or to Hobbes, who reminds us that between leaders and followers, the differences in strength are not as great as usually assumed: the bastard without an army Jon Snow tames Fortune and becomes the "King in the North." The alcoholic dwarf Tyrion, whom his family hates because of his attraction for places of ill repute, becomes Queen Daenerys' prime minister. Or Mance Ryder, the former deserter of the Night's Watch, who embodies the only credible leader in the story because he is the only one who is elected without behaving like an autocrat. At the same time, Melisandre sees in Stannis “the prince who was promised” when he loses the military battle by basing his strategy on beginner’s mistakes.

But it should perhaps be pointed out here that, after all, the most didactic philosopher is one of the key figures, Lord Varys, the master of whisperers. If he does not shy away from any manipulation, if he is not lacking in obsequiousness, he keeps in mind what everyone seems to have forgotten: the common good and the interest of all. On the subject of power, he concludes that it “resides where men think it resides. It is a decoy, a shadow and a wall. A very small man can cast an immense shadow.” Here is a statement that all those involved in, and observing, public life should ponder.

To parents worried that their offspring have become obsessed with such a crude program, let me offer a message of consolation by assuring them that, all in all, this saga is proving to be a surprising learning device with much to teach us about the very foundations of the exercise of power.

Only Those Who Play Their Cards Right Are Trustworthy

Nassim Nicholas Taleb, *Skin in the Game: Hidden Asymmetries in Daily Life* (Random House, 2017).

When a sales manager says of one of the salespeople in her team that she has “confidence in him,” should this statement be considered in terms of morality or competence? Is she confident that this colleague will not sell at a loss, will respect the terms of the contract, will not lie about the real qualities of the product? Or does it mean that she has confidence in them to take the company’s results to the highest level, in terms of the volume of turnover generated by their commercial activity? Perhaps this “trust” is a mixture of the two, faith in the honesty of these employees and credit given to their efficiency in carrying out these tasks.

Essentially, argues Nassim Nicholas Taleb in his latest essay, managers do not truly know the difference, as it is so delicate “in the real world, to dissociate ethics from knowledge.” This is why, according to this unclassifiable author, born in Lebanon, of Greek Orthodox Christian culture, a former Wall Street trader who became a successful essayist after making his fortune, the only moral criterion to be taken into account is whether these salespeople are in a position to pay for the effects, good or bad, of their action. Implied: if a manager or employee does not suffer the consequences of his actions, then you can expect him to behave badly, at least without ethical considerations of any kind. It is by virtue of this situation that, in the author’s view, you can never trust someone whose future depends, not on the risks he or she incurs for his or her actions, but only on the “professional assessments” of a superior. For Taleb, if society progresses, it is thanks to those who take risks, are accountable . . . in short, those with skin in the game.

This radical approach, to say the least, to professional ethics bears the hallmark of an author who made a name for himself with his book *The Black Swan* in 2007, one year before the financial crisis, which showed that in the evolution of human societies, it is always unexpected events that make History. A timely warning, as the financial crisis of 2008 erupted a few months later. He made his mark a few years later with a second essay, "Antifragile," which showed that the least fragile organizations were the most agile (i.e., those that know how to strategically take advantage of delicate situations). But this self-proclaimed libertarian, linked to a political philosophy opposed to an increased role for the state, could not stop there. With this new opus, he reveals the ethical side of his project.

It therefore attacks here those who do not suffer from the decisions they take or make others take. He calls them "interventionistas," among whom we find Bernard-Henri Lévy as well as Thomas Piketty or Paul Krugman, these fast thinkers who would never pay for their errors of analysis and their positions, who would never be "subjected to the filter and the discipline of putting their skin on the line." To support this unreserved argument, he relies on the first known ethical register, the Code of Hammurabi,[36] which states, "If a man accuses another man and charges him with homicide, but cannot bring proof against him, his accuser shall be killed."

To this book, which is full of philosophy but unfortunately misquotes Pascal and invokes history by putting "the spirit of sacrifice" before "the spirit of enjoyment," we might reply that the spirit of geometry does not always prevail over the spirit of finesse. Especially in moral matters, which are the subject of this book, where geometry and statistical science do not always have their place.

The Entrepreneur, a Contemporary "Adventurer"?

Jean-Baptiste Frossard, *L'aventure—Homer, Jankélévich, Conrad* (PUF, 2017.)

Are entrepreneurs adventurers, perhaps even the last true adventurers of late modernity? It is often under this recklessly glorious label that one presents the person who sets out to create a business. In fact, it is in the adventurous mode that Joseph Schumpeter, the thinker of creative destruction, conceived the capitalist entrepreneur.

Is entrepreneurship, something more and more young people are doing or wish to do, really the last adventure of the century? Is the risk so great and the result so uncertain? We know that most newly created companies disappear in their first three years, whereas today, "going on a trip," even to the remotest parts of the planet, is no longer the risky endeavor that it was in Magellan's time, or more recently, in the time of Alexandra David-Néel and Paul-Émile Victor.

Aventure, a beautiful concept that provides the title for this work by Jean-Baptiste Frossard, to which is appended a new edition with commentary by Arnaud Sorosina of Vladimir Jankélévitch's text titled *L'aventure, l'ennui et le sérieux* (Adventure, Boredom and Seriousness). An opportunity to reacquaint ourselves with the work of this French philosopher, who died in 1985, and his views on the theme of adventure:

> The adventurous man represents a real lifestyle, whereas an adventurer is someone professionally engaged in adventures; for the latter, the priority is not to undertake adventures, but to earn money; and if he knew a way to earn money without adventures, he would choose that way; adventures are his stock in trade, and he regards risk in much the same way that a grocer regards mustard.

Here we have two very different ways of thinking about adventure, and particularly the entrepreneurial adventure. These two types of entrepreneur are implicitly described here.

On the one hand, wandering mercenaries, using all the possibilities of trickery, deception if necessary, to achieve their goal (i.e., their interest), who live their action as a rite and according to the determinations of a system. On the other hand, entrepreneurs who value adventures over "ventures," who consider adventure to be an end in and of itself, where nothing or little is determined in advance. Such adventurers willingly accept a certain gratuitousness, a taste for the possible, for the beautiful gesture and for style. Adventurous entrepreneurs are aristocrats reconciled to the unpredictability of time. For adventurous individuals, the true and authentic activity is, to use a learned word, "self-rewarding": it carries within itself its own reward.

This second unusual figure in the entrepreneurial adventure is interesting to meditate on for at least two reasons. First, isn't it the mark of an entrepreneur to be able to withstand uncertainty in a negotiation, in a takeover, in a new launch? Schumpeter pointed out that an entrepreneur is someone who knows how to break the routine but who very quickly finds herself thwarted by bureaucratic systems that make it difficult for novelty to emerge. From this point of view, adventurous entrepreneurship offers an alternative, because it is first and foremost the art of beginnings, or rather of eternal restarts.

Second, this other figure in the entrepreneurial adventure is the one who takes seriously the unforeseen nature of creation and organizational inventiveness. In the face of adversity, defeat, and surprise, only an ability to accept the unsuspected, the unplanned, can allow new ideas, new know-how, and new projects to emerge. That is why an entrepreneurial adventure worthy of its name is also, and above all, an ethical and aesthetic experience of openness to the world and to the possibility of a "maybe."

Myths and Realities of Self-Entrepreneurship

Sarah Abdelnour, *Moi, petite entreprise. Les autoentrepreneurs, de l'utopie à la réalité*[37] (PUF, 2017).

Faced with the risks engendered by Uberization of our economy, and the corresponding fall in the number of salaried jobs in the traditional sense, several responses are emerging. Perhaps the most plausible goes something like this: each of us will have to become an entrepreneur at least once in our working lives.

Sociologist Sarah Abdelnour here examines the conditions surrounding the creation of the status of auto-entrepreneur, or rather micro-entrepreneur, as it has been called in France since 2016. In parallel, this book analyzes from a sociological point of view the exponential development of new labor regulations, which have led to more than a million people switching to self-employment, freed from the constraints generally associated with salaried engagement. This regulation will be developed in the future, as Emmanuel Macron, in his previous functions as minister of the economy, was keen to triple the activity and income thresholds currently applicable to this legal framework.

Is this new regime keeping all its promises? Reading Abdelnour's survey, we discover first that self-entrepreneurship is not a French invention: in 2003, the Germans developed the "Ich-AG" system, while the Spanish four years later imagined the status of trabajadores autonomos.

We also learn that the permanent "project mode" that characterizes these activities contains a kind of paradox: certainly, the administrative procedures for registering the activity are simplified, but this only lasts for a short time because very quickly the bureaucracy takes over. The micro-entrepreneur soon learns the hard way that she must spend a significant part of her working time solving paperwork problems that, in a regular business, would be partly the responsibility of people dedicated to these tasks. Finally, nine out of ten micro-entrepreneurs have incomes below the minimum wage, which may appear disappointing in view of the hopes of remuneration that this "unleashing" of professional energy was supposed to generate.

But the principal interest of this study lies elsewhere. First, it clearly shows that the scheme usually covers a transitional period, during which the entrepreneur is looking for paid employment. Moreover, and this is more surprising in view of the initial conclusions, "it is therefore clear that the scheme has earned the unanimous support of the users we met, which transcends their differences in political views." Could this be a third way, between the financial capital of shareholders and the labor force of salaried individuals? Would this book, therefore, be a statement of a new spirit of capitalism, almost twenty years after the publication of the book of that name by Luc Boltanski and Ève Chiapello?

In fact, the merit of this essay is that it gives us a glimpse of an ongoing transformation of the economy, and the choice of society more generally induced by these developments, without falling prey to sometimes simplistic mythology that informs many articles in the general press dealing with these issues. The author shows that between part-time employees, small bosses, micro-entrepreneurs, intermittent workers, self-employed managers, and those taking over craft businesses, to give just a few examples, the boundaries of popular entrepreneurship and the names with which it is associated are constantly changing.

Mediocrats

Alain Deneault, *Mediocracy: The Politics of the Extreme Centre*, trans. Catherine Brown (Between the Lines, 2018).

> Put away those complicated books; the accounting books will do the trick. Don't be proud, witty, or even at ease; you may appear arrogant. Ease your passions; they are frightening. Above all, no "good ideas"; the shredder is full of them. That piercing look that worries you: widen it and relax your lips; you have to think softly and show it, talk about your ego by reducing it to a minimum; you have to be able to fit in. Times have changed . . . the mediocre have taken over.

And so Alain Deneault, a Quebecois philosopher and author of numerous books, sets the tone from which he rarely departs over the course of this short essay. This criticism of mediocratic power must be understood from two angles: bemoaning a lack of quality, certainly, but also implacably analyzing the rise of "averageness" in leadership circles.

For Deneault, access to dominant positions is only possible for those who accept to "play the game" of the system—that is, the card of mimicry and reproduction of the dominant system. To obtain a position or an advancement, it would therefore be advisable to follow the same path, paved with services rendered, servility toward the powerful, feigned humility, and the use of language impoverished by the usual expressions of the corporate rhetoric in force. The maneuver will be "dressed in hollow words"; in the opposite case, "we will drive out the spirits that do not participate in duplicity, and this, of course, in a mediocre way, through denial, denial and resentment."

This study, in addition to the section devoted to "average" as access to employment, looks at mediocrity as a management principle, the very opposite of excellence, which is nevertheless constantly being postulated in this field. The fault lies with Taylorism, which defended the principle of standardization in industry and the principle of the interchangeability of individuals on the production line thanks to the skills system. Employment is not an opportunity to create; it has little by little become a "means" of subsistence.

From this vivid and subversive demonstration, one must retain the ferocious and often just charge of "normalcy," that false pretense that, under the guise of imitation and reproduction, gives itself a form of soft banality as the horizon and principle of government. Because innovation and commitment, management's greatest promises,[38] always come at the price of risk taking and a certain break with past values.

On the other hand, I am less inclined to agree with the author's denunciation of the prevailing principle of "averageness." In his essay "Average Is Over," the American economist Tyler Cowen shows that this principle of "averageness," or mediocrity, is bound for extinction. The world is split into two camps: those—more and more numerous—who are at the mercy of new technologies, and those who take full advantage of them. Average is increasingly looked down upon, in favor of a polarization between small jobs and elite jobs that is far more worrying for the supposedly hyper-connected society.

But isn't there a middle way between criticizing mediocrity and proclaiming the death of "averageness?" Couldn't we just split the difference?

A Leader Must Know How to Disobey

Frédéric Gros, *Disobey! A Philosophy of Resistance* (Verso, 2020).

Are we able to say no? Faced with an authority that compels us to go against our principles, our conscience, our instinct, can we put up firm, definitive resistance? Each of us believes that we are strong enough to have the courage to oppose, and the natural assumption seems to be that indocility, insubordination, even outright rebellion, are appropriate responses that everyone can use to make their voices heard. Disobedience is the ethical and political response that is always needed to challenge and shake things up.

And yet, as the philosopher Frédéric Gros remarks, it should be noted that the recalcitrant are rare and the obedient numerous. Easy though it may be to agree on good reasons to revolt, says this professor of political thought at the IEP (Paris School of International Affairs), we prefer the comfort of resignation. The price of insubordination is simply too high. If one obeys, it is because it is inconvenient to disobey, but it is also out of habit: in the eyes of the submissive, the subordinate, the conformist, or simply the consenting, there is always a good reason to obey, even if that reason turns out to be absurd or revolting.

In this essay, the author also offers a critical reading of Milgram's experiments, which highlighted the risks of blind obedience within a group. He also returns to the case of Adolf Eichmann, the Nazi war criminal who declared at the time of his trial that he had been content to follow the prescriptions of his military hierarchy. "He had a job to do, orders to carry out," writes Gros, and he accepted "to be punished, but only within this framework. His task was to see that the trains left on time. He considered it "purely a logistical problem." Chilling.

Gros's position is that the possibility of disobedience is also the condition of our responsibility. In this respect, disobedience is a non-delegable virtue, which belongs to us in its own right, which we cannot give up to anyone else. Faithful in this to Michel Foucault, on whose thought he is an eminent specialist, the author speaks to us here of the relationship we have with ourselves, of a form of active resistance that resides entirely in the act of thinking.

Thinking, in fact, is often reasoning against oneself, against one's own beliefs. And this is why his essay is important for managers: without the ability to question their habits and agreed ideas, mimicry always prevails in an organization. Yet the role of management, faced with the systems of constraint and imitation that are still prevalent in companies, is precisely to oppose an imaginative force, which is also a form of resistance to the do-nothing attitudes that represent such a risk to the survival, or even the renewal, of any collective project.

But a limit to this exercise remains: it sometimes happens that insubordination becomes a posture, a rule, a habit, an addiction no nobler in itself than the obedience here called into question. In short, disobedience can become as hard a drug as obedience. This is why the antidote is in what Gros reminds us: disobedience or obedience should only be by conviction and consent, rather than by habit, as Blaise Pascal reminds us in this well-known pensée:

> It is your own satisfaction, and the constant path of reason, and not of others, that should make you believe.

To acquiesce does not necessarily mean to resign, and to disobey does not always mean to innovate. The big yes of consent is not necessarily less important than the big no of disobedience. As far as today's so-called agile organizations are concerned, they certainly need both.

Social Networks, or "The Invasion of Imbeciles"

Maurizio Ferraris, L'imbécilité est une chose sérieuse[39] (PUF, 2017).

Social networks have provided a soapbox to legions of idiots who previously only raised their voices at the bar after a few glasses, without causing any harm to the community. They were immediately silenced, but now they have the same right to speak as a Nobel Prize winner. It's an invasion of imbeciles.

A year before his death, the Italian intellectual Umberto Eco made this untimely statement to an audience of journalists on a day when he was being presented with an academic award. This appropriation of the public debate by idiots, this mass imbecility made inevitable by social media, sets the tone for this essay by Maurizio Ferraris, author of a notable study on our relationship with our mobile phones. This time he tackles a problem not of medium but of content, namely imbecility, that "burden of civilization," that form of unintelligence that gives man his main characteristic. Etymologically, imbecility means "deprived of a stick"—that is, deprived of help, deprived of tools: man in his native, original state.

Ferraris agrees with Umberto Eco, adding, however, that social media not only allows propagation of imbecility, but also production of it: he thus evokes the example revealed on YouTube of Yves Leterme, a Belgian politician who sang the wrong national anthem, singing "La Marseillaise" rather than "La Brabançonne," without this in any way changing the result of the election because the candidate became one year later prime minister of his country.

"Foolishness," Ferraris explains, "is the hallmark of modernity because, with the potential offered by the modern world, the stupid is revealed better than in any other era, more contemplative and more silent." Note that our author, a philosopher by trade, does not spare members of his profession, who also take it for granted. He cites Wittgenstein, who selected his students at the entrance to his Cambridge seminar in the manner of a nightclub bouncer ("You, yes. You, no!"). He also recalls the bracing example of Kant "writing himself a note to 'forget about Lampe,' hoping to enable himself to forget about a servant who had been dear to him, but whom he had been obliged to dismiss over suspicions of dishonesty."

Not even the greatest minds are immune to bouts of foolishness. Not Napoleon, nor even Socrates, who believed that ignorance was the source of evil. If we repeat the same mistakes, it is not because of ignorance or weakness of will; it is simply because we are fools in the first place. In the business world, this means that "whatever we do, we will make mistakes," and we will make them mechanically, without thinking about it, out of habit, sometimes even repeating them over and over again.

But, then, where will our redemption come from? Should we, for example, practice neural reinforcement, as the specialists in artificial intelligence seem to advise? This is not the path chosen by our author, who finally begins to warm to his subject somewhat. "Let us acknowledge that discovering that the lider maximo is a fool can sometimes have more emancipating effects than a revolution," he writes. The naivety, for example, of entrepreneurship, our candor in the face of the possibility of changing the world, all this contributes to the dynamism of human life in general and of organizations in particular. Even in our weaknesses, recognized as such, in our simplicity of spirit described by Dostoyevsky in *The Idiot*, there is a nobility that sometimes exceeds the small calculations of the cleverest among us. For in the end, we are all half fools. And it is less worrying to become aware of this than to pretend to ignore it.

Are All "No!"s Equal?

Vincent Delecroix, Non! de l'esprit de révolte[40] (Autrement, 2018).

"I would prefer not to." So goes the unexpected response given by Bartleby, a simple clerk in a notary's office who suddenly refuses to obey some of his boss's most innocuous requests. This famous short story, written by Herman Melville and named after his hero, fascinated philosophers throughout the twentieth century. Perhaps it is time for managers to take an interest in it, too.

This enigmatic refusal to obey is problematic for management, which is defined by a power of constraint: Bartleby, a small employee with no apparent stature, suddenly reminds his boss that, as Diderot put it, "no man has received from nature the right to command others."

This resistance to power also offers a glimpse of freedom rejecting constraints, to the point where, tired of the conflict, the boss ends up not asking anything at all from the recalcitrant employee. For the refusal in question is not pure and simple, hence the difficulties we have in translating such a phrase in any language. Bartleby's expression has become iconic, representing his passive resistance to hierarchical power without ever clearly revealing his intentions: is he angry at his employer or at humanity as a whole? Does he want to make the voice of protest heard or, on the contrary, to remain discreet and measured? Might we even see him as a pioneering advocate of the so-called liberated company?[41] In any case, we know that his opposition is founded upon a refusal, a principled no.

For Vincent Delecroix, who teaches philosophy of religion at the École pratique des hautes études in Paris, this refusal is a sign of a freedom defined less by the power to do than by the power not to want. "Being unable to not do something," he explains, "would be a real nightmare." Giving up something that you have the power may thus be seen as a symbol of freedom.

In short, real power may in fact be a negative capability. But the subtitle of this work ("On the spirit of revolt") may be somewhat misleading, because Delecroix's philosophy of "no" tries as much as possible to get out of the spirit of contradiction, indignation, or systematic resentment. No is not always the answer. It is not a question of saying no to everything, which would be meaningless:

> As Wittgenstein pointed out, hinges must be fixed for the door to turn: in other words, certain things must be beyond doubt for one to doubt . . . For the No to be practiced, something must be beyond its reach.

The no in question is "restive," ethical, and fair. Justice, explains Delecroix, is best expressed in opposition to injustice.

Through a series of examples, the author develops his concept. In the sciences, for example, progress is made from new representations opposed to the old ones. In the arts, it is the same: an artistic work is always a way of opposing the existing world, of expressing a certain refusal. As for the man or woman who "develops his or her business, or the factory manager who sees his or her industry prosper," to use Bergson's expression, is it not ultimately the same? Entrepreneurship is often about rejecting and surpassing preexisting business models. Is innovation first and foremost a repudiation of old systems of thought that have failed?

It is almost as if in art, in politics, and even in literature or management, one must first, as Delecroix urges us to do, "try to find your own No."

In Defense of Intestinal Management

Antonio Damasio, *The Strange Order of Things: Life, Feeling, and the Making of Cultures* (Pantheon Books, 2018).

Are our organizations, particularly our governance structures, the product of reasoned calculation or a living, constantly updated expression of our sensibility?

The primordial philosophical question of mind versus body (which best reveals who we are and what we do?) can be transposed to the domain of human creations—our businesses and institutions, for example. Antonio Damasio, a professor at the University of Southern California and a world-renowned researcher in neurobiology, has no doubt about it: ultimately, our feelings always guide our intellect:

> At first glance, the subject of governance might seem foreign to that of biology, I am aware of this. But it is not. Governance requires long processes of negotiation, which are directly linked to the biology of affects. . . . It is impossible to escape it.

The ideas that Damasio produces here revolve around what he calls homeostasis—that is, a regulatory capacity that allows any system to maintain itself over time, despite the plurality of its constituent parts. Stasis in ancient Greek means "to stand upright." In the case of an organization, considered as an organism, homeostasis—a term with cybernetic emphasis—represents the cornerstone of its unity, a sort of milieu where those forces that constantly betray it, changing strategies, for example; and those that reaffirm its own DNA, its profession identity, for instance, are permanently intertwined. Homeostasis can thus be viewed as an organizational response to the "contingency factors" dear to Henry Mintzberg and to environmental transformations.

However, Damasio argues, "organizational homeostasis" is necessarily informed by our feelings, thanks to which we trigger our best faculties of adaptation, evolution, and progress. Our feelings, our joys, and our sufferings are thus, in a way, the "assistants" of homeostasis. They constantly provide the information it needs. The body and the nervous system thus always take precedence over the mind, affect trumps reason, or, to put it more bluntly, our intestines lord it over our ego. The reference to the intestines, to our "enteral nervous system," may come as a surprise, but Damasio explains in a few pages how they are in a way our second brain, made up of 100,000 billion bacteria. These micro-organisms, which appeared nearly four billion years ago, are intelligent, the author marvels, able to communicate, endowed with memory, and incredibly capable of organizing and defending themselves. For the author, the strategies of these unicellular organisms "prefigure" our own ways of organizing and defending ourselves.

So, what lessons can we learn from these notions of homeostasis and the "second brain" to which we are generally unaccustomed in management? First, they give credence to the theories that make motivation the heart of managerial success. Management would be precisely this function of maintaining homeostasis in its upper echelon. But this is never more so than when we experience joy; for example, when we create something. Damasio also reasserts the principle that the first aim of human organizations is always self-preservation, on a model that is both Darwinian—of natural selection—and Spinozist: the Dutch philosopher, indeed, considered that our deepest motivation consists in an instinct of preservation, which he called the conatus.

Nevertheless, the author admits that the analyses in this book, while enthusiastically demonstrating that bodies and minds are immersed in the same bath of life, stumble over a lack of explanations. The risk of "biologizing" management would be to reduce human life to a representation, to an object like any other, and not to an inexplicable experience that is the source of all our possible experiences. A certain modesty should, therefore, be maintained, as the anti-Cartesian Damasio explains in conclusion. In the pure sciences, too, one must retain the capacity to doubt everything. One's presumptions, of course, and particularly one's prejudices.

NOTES

1. M. Alvesson and H. Willmott, eds., *Studying Management Critically*, op. cit.
2. J. Bouveresse, "Les managers peuvent-ils avoir un idéal?" in *Essais, II. L'époque, la mode, la morale, la satire* (Marseille, Agone, 2001), 165–87.
3. G. Deslandes, "Philosophy and Management Sciences: Towards a Poetics of Managerial Action? Orientation de recherche et questions d'enseignement," *Diotime 51*, no. 1 (2012), online.
4. J. Bouveresse, "Les managers pouvezt-ils avoir un idéal," op. cit., 172.
5. G. Deslandes, *Critique de la condition managériale*, op. cit.
6. *The Merchants and the Temple. Christian society and the virtuous circle of wealth, from the Middle Ages to the Modern Era.* Original title: *I mercanti e il tempio. La società cristiana e il circolo virtuoso della ricchezza fra Medioevo ed età moderna.*
7. *Industrial Religion: Monasteries, manufactories and factories.*
8. *Mammuth*, dir. Gustave Kervern and Benoît Délépine (GMT Productions/No Money Productions, 2010).
9. When the world turned into numbers.
10. A term first used by Pitirim Sorokin to denounce the harmful temptation to quantify everything about our psychological and social reality.
11. cf. G. Deslandes, *Critique de la condition managériale* (Paris: PUF, 2016).
12. Celestial computing.
13. Heidegger and the question of management.
14. What is to be done with idiots? To avoid being one yourself.
15. Creativity at work.
16. Cited in the book on p. 20.
17. Employment is dead, long live work! Interview with Ariel Kyrou.
18. See, for instance, https://www.youtube.com/watch?v=R5lZPWNFizQ.
19. www.arsindustrialis.org.
20. Translated from French.
21. *Wall Street* (United States, 20th Century Fox, 1987).
22. J. Jankélévitch, *L'aventure, l'ennui, le sérieux*, text presented by Arnaud Sorosina (Paris: Flammarion, 2017–2018). This book is reviewed hereunder, cf. p. 55.
23. Fragilité.
24. B. J. Avolio and B. M. Bass, "Transformational leadership, charisma and beyond," work paper, State University of New York, Binghamton, 1985.
25. C. L. Pearce and J. A. Conger, *Shared Leadership: Reframing the Hows and Whys of Leadership* (Thousand Oaks, CA: Sage, 2003).

26. M. Uhl-Bien, "Relational Leadership and Gender: From Hierarchy to Relationality," *in* P. Werhane and M. Painter-Morland, eds., *Leadership, Gender and Organization* (Dordrecht: Springer, 2011).

27. A. Deneault, *Mediocracy: The Politics of the Extreme Centre*, trans. Catherine Brown (Between the Line, 2018).

28. Discussed later in this book.

29. How to govern a kingly people? A new treatise on political art.

30. Vulgarity and modernity.

31. Take. Birth of an elementary social practice.

32. Who will take over? The great apes, politicians or robots.

33. *Stages on the Path of Life*, Editions de l'Orante, vol. 9, 214 (see also vol. 6, 244).

34. *House of Cards.* Crime in politics.

35. These questions form the basis of a special issue of *Philosophie Magazine*, including contributions from Laurence Devillairs, Mathieu Potte-Bonneville, Raphaël Enthoven, and Tristan Garcia, with reference to this important chapter in the history of serial fiction.

36. Most French people are unaware of the fact that this imposing gray and black stele is on display in the Louvre museum.

37. Me, small business. Self-entrepreneurs, from utopia to reality.

38. See G. Deslandes, *Critique de la condition managériale*, op. cit.

39. Foolishness is a serious thing.

40. No! of the spirit of revolt.

41. B. Carney and I. Geetz, *Freedom, Inc.: How Corporate Liberation Unleashes Employee Potential and Business Performance* (Somme Valley House, 2016).

Chapter 2

Critiques of the "Capitalocene"

This second chapter leads us to a series of reflections on the context in which management and leadership are exercised today. As I see it, these two manners of acting upon the world necessarily require a solid understanding of that world. This is why the works commented on here present, in the form of a somewhat impressionistic kaleidoscope, an overview of the current state of Europe and of capitalism, constituting what we might call a morality of worry.

Against this backdrop, the contextual mutations that organizations face are certainly multifaceted, but two seem to me to be of particular structural importance: globalization and the ecological question on the one hand, and the digital revolution on the other.

FROM GLOBAL CHANGES TO THE ADVENT OF *HOMO ŒCOLOGICUS*

In this first section, therefore, I consider globalization and its consequences by starting with a twofold inaugural question: one proposed by the jurist Mireille Delmas-Marty on our possibilities for collective action in the face of the complexity of organizations; and one by demographer and historian Emmanuel Todd, who has studied the differentiation of family systems to answer, based on a sketch of human history, this ambitious question: Where do we stand?

For the philosopher Régis Debray and the political scientist Ivan Krastev, the evolution of human history requires us to rethink Europe's position in the world: while the former argues that Europe is no longer one of the world's great civilizations, the latter contends that our continent must urgently confront, at the risk of disappearing, the problem of populism(s), even if this involves using the same means as its adversaries. This possible disappearance could just as well find its source in the thesis of the philosopher Eric Sadin, in this other form of colonization that he calls "siliconization." With this concept, he denounces California's ideological victory over other models of development and the very probable cultural domination of techno-liberalism. However, this domination worries and at the same time emboldens critics, such as economist Raj Patel and historian Jason Moore, who are campaigning for an "ecology of repair."

To say no, however, can call the attention of the actors of globalization in very different directions: we can observe several of them from a reflection on the notion of "commons," which is increasingly attracting the attention of the social sciences, and on that of "innervation" rather than innovation, based on a political reflection on the consequences of the rise of the immaterial economy. I also reserve a place for the renewal of the economy of development with the analyses of Mohammad Yunus, the most media-friendly proponent of social business, but also for new philosophical proposals, from thinkers such as Timothy Morton and Baptiste Monsaingeon, to renew ecological thinking. Finally, I give the floor to Bruno Latour, one of France's most influential intellectuals, who died in 2022. He raised the Earth to the level of a new philosophical concept, reminding us that it is precisely Europe's responsibility to put the planet at the heart of economic and political decisions.

The Art of Sailing in the Globalized Ocean

Mireille Delmas-Marty, *Aux quatre vents du monde. Petit guide de navigation sur l'océan de la mondialisation* (Seuil, 2016).

Faced with global challenges—migration, mass unemployment, terrorism, and global warming, not to mention the other perils and calamities (COVID-19) added to this litany on a daily basis—is proposing real solutions the only possible response? Politicians constantly strive in this direction, but the scant success they enjoy appears to offer further confirmation of the "tragedy of the 3Cs": when a system exceeds a certain threshold of complexity, it cannot be both complete and coherent. Indeed, in complex systems, as set theorists have established, we cannot have coherence and completeness at the same time. Is this not, at heart, the essential tragedy of public policy? Are we condemned to impotence, skepticism, and inaction?

This is not the opinion of Mireille Delmas-Marty, who offers this brief guide to navigating the oceans of globalization. For the author, a specialist in criminal sciences who passed away in February 2022, and who formerly held a chair in comparative legal studies at the Collège de France, humanity has entered the "doldrums." This name designates an area of the Atlantic dreaded by sailors because the wind can blow in any direction, or stop blowing altogether, leaving sailors stuck for weeks on end. According to Delmas-Marty, this terrifying zone is the point on the map where we are today, condemned to "let ourselves be carried along" when the winds are favorable, to "wander in the face of headwinds," and to "survive the dead calm."

Moving beyond this metaphor, which will surely delight yachting enthusiasts, the author proposes a legal response as a compass in the face of the current crises. This compass differentiates between the four prevailing winds of globalization: freedom, security, competition, and cooperation. As she explains, "this compass could also indicate . . . other winds, such as the spirit of innovation between freedom and competition; the spirit of exclusion between competition and security; the spirit of conservation between security and cooperation; or the spirit of integration between cooperation and freedom."

Delmas-Marty thus sketches out a new vision of international law designed to avoid catalepsy or drowning and to give human beings back their sense of initiative by resisting the lure of autopilot. Her analysis is indispensable but essentially legalistic, and this is at once its strength and its limit. "Sweet justice bounded by a river," as Pascal might have put it, reminding us that questions of society are, first and foremost, played out on an ethical and political level. The imaginative forces of law have neither the capacity to transform the present custom nor the authority of the sovereign, as we saw when Donald Trump summarily pulled the United States out of the Paris climate agreement.

All of which means that, when we are invited to vote, we must certainly choose the best crew to get out of the doldrums, but without losing sight of the tragedy of the 3Cs: any affirmative choice, unfortunately, includes its dose of sacrifices and concessions, the price of action. We can vote better, or at least less badly, if we can bear that in mind.

Anthropology and Intercultural Management

Emmanuel Todd, *Lineages of Modernity: A History of Humanity from the Stone Age to Homo Americanus* (Polity Press, 2019).

Starting from a question ("where are we?") that is, after all, banal, the demographer and historian Emmanuel Todd poses a problem that seems very difficult to answer. Thomas Friedman's best-selling book *The World Is Flat*, published more than a decade ago, nevertheless hinted at an answer in the form of strong cooperation between peoples, rather than the divergent phenomena that seem to be gaining ground today. And yet, the world appears more buckled than ever: how else can we describe our era, made up of major challenges to our models, global warming, political uncertainties, but also prodigious medical and technological advances? What are we to make of the current events that, from our Western control centers, we can no longer explain, such as the nonrecognition of homosexuality or the decline in human rights in too many countries?

Even restricting ourselves to a purely economic analysis, the situation of the world today seems thoroughly incomprehensible. Todd explains that the steamroller of globalization, as described by economists and others, is not aware of what is happening at the lower level, which determines everything—namely, those structures that are far more decisive than the economy, such as religion, the nation, and, even more so, family systems.

In this book, the author undertakes an ambitious work of historical reconstruction, ranging from homo sapiens to Donald Trump, from Judaism to Christianity, the construction of Europe and the West. This panorama of different anthropological mutations is based on the differentiation of family systems that exist in an ancestral way, and of which Todd proposes a typology: for example, with the egalitarian nuclear family as found in France; the family of origin that designates a single heir as in Japan or Korea; the exogamous communitarian family as in China; or even, requiring a greater imaginative leap for us Europeans, the nuclear family with temporary matriarchal co-residence as in Thailand.

His thesis is that our collective unconscious bears the mark of these family systems and that, without them, we are incapable of understanding what is happening to us politically and geostrategically: the return of the so-called Great Man as well as the opposition to gender equality in many countries of the world, or Brexit. The essayist also adds to this list the over-consumption and intrinsic violence of American society, which for him refers "to the model of predation that characterised (in this part of the world) the original man."

In the end, this anthropological and historical analysis is an invitation to consider an important lesson in intercultural management. If we want to better understand the current mutations of the globalized economy, let us begin by reducing the distance between the economy and other fields of knowledge, in particular the study of local customs that serve to show us that a homogenous humanity is an unreachable horizon, a whim that can only amplify conflicts and culture shocks, because, as Todd explains, there is no absolute identity but always relative identities that exist in relation to one other :

France only really began to exist, in the fourteenth century, as a result of its conflict with England; white Americans existed only in relation to blacks, Greeks only in relation to barbarians, Athenians in relation to Spartans, Christians in relation to Jews and Pagans.

In short, no one has ever been built without external references.

The Destiny of Europe in the Age of "Rhinoceritis"

Ivan Krastev, *After Europe* (Philadelphia: University of Pennsylvania Press, 2017).

Are European citizens suffering from "rhinoceritis," the disease invented by the playwright Eugène Ionesco? In his *Rhinoceros*, the sudden appearance of these three-ton mammals causes a chain reaction among the population, to the point where everyone ends up thinking they are a ferocious beast. At the beginning, of course, everyone is afraid: "We can't afford to have our cats crushed by rhinos, or anything else!" exclaims the grocer. But very quickly, as if by a trail of gunpowder, through mimesis or through fear, everyone starts to find it normal. Ionesco, a playwright of Romanian origin who became a French academician, warned us as early as 1959 against the ever-present risk of extremism, even when it appears to be a minority concern.

This image is taken up in a new essay by Ivan Krastev of Vienna's Institute for Human Sciences. Europeans today are said to be caught in a double contradiction: resentment of the meritocratic elites but recognition of the continent's stability in terms of security, on the one hand; and on the other, a rise in national and even regional sentiments, all while collaboration against terrorism between the member states of the Union is more effective than ever before. In the words of Krastev, "Europeans are living in fear of disintegration when they share a common destiny more than ever." The uncertainties and difficulties encountered by the British in leaving the Union hardly prove him wrong.

For this increasingly influential political scientist, the risk that Europe—along with its court of justice and the right of its people to move without constraints, and of course to elect their representatives—could simply disintegrate is very real. Western Europeans pretend to be unaware of this, while Eastern Europeans, who have not forgotten the Iron Curtain, cannot afford the luxury of unconsciousness. "In the event of a major security crisis," Krastev asserts, "public opinion in at least three EU countries—Bulgaria, Greece, and Slovenia—would seek assistance from Russia, not the West."

It is, therefore, a matter for concern: this era of resentment offers a unique opportunity for populist parties to make their voices heard, as they promise to "stand by the people" when the elites jump ship, as is the case in Bulgaria, a country that the author knows well. This perilous situation, theorized by the British sociologist Michael Young, puts European liberal democracy on high alert while the migration crisis further widens the gap between cosmopolitan and clan mentalities.

In short, Europe is facing its "Galapagos syndrome": this phenomenon was used to describe the superiority of Japanese smartphones over all others at the beginning of the 3G era, which nevertheless failed to sell overseas because other countries did not have the technology required to make these Japanese products workable. Today, Europe is a bit like that: its strong points—secularism, postmodernity, openness to the world—do not seem to make it a model for anyone, despite its supposedly more "advanced" model in terms of democracy.

In conclusion, Krastev proposes to "disarm" the populists by being receptive to some of their concerns. This requires a degree of political courage, reminding ourselves that otherness is always a good thing and that ultimately, "we must hold on." He thus takes the path proposed by Machiavelli, the Florentine strategist, of never giving up until one knows everything about one's own destiny.

Allow me to add that if we are to finally break out of the present mire of Euroskepticism, what we need is nothing less than a proper realization of the geostrategic stakes on the part of each European. And let us not forget that if the antiheroes in Ionesco's play are transformed into perissodactyl mammals, it is primarily because they are entrapped by a narrow conception of identity, which they fail to exchange for a broader perspective.

Total Siliconization

Éric Sadin, *La Siliconisation du monde*[1] (L'Échappée, 2016).

The colonization of the world (i.e., the taking of political power of one country by another) has been followed by the siliconization of the world (i.e., the economic, technological, and cultural takeover of all the world's countries by a region in the western United States). For Éric Sadin, author of this essay on an unprecedented form of colonization, there is no doubt that it is just as frightening as the previous one, precisely because we are blind to both its ideological content and the devastating consequences it has for our own ways of living in Europe, Asia, Africa, and elsewhere.

Silicon Cape Town in South Africa, Bangalore, the Indian Silicon Valley, Sydney's silicon beach, among many other examples, show that the California system has become dominant even in the way countries grasp the need to innovate. It is as if the silicon victory were total and left no room for any serious organizational or managerial alternative to challenge its development model.

This widespread ideology, emanating, of course, from Silicon Valley itself, was built on a mixture of total liberalism and an unbridled taste for technological advances, but also, and this is less well known, on philosophical foundations that are at once Zen, pantheistic, and positivist. A cocktail that may come as a surprise but is even now transforming the ways in which we communicate, shop, do business, and make decisions. Siliconization works on the model of total evangelization: it is a question of spreading a message with a universal vocation, on a scale never achieved in the past, because it is a system that encompasses all dimensions of life.

For Sadin, the installation of sensors in all our professional and personal spaces, our toothbrushes, our supposedly intelligent mirrors, our glasses, is leaving us increasingly reduced to reacting to signals, living under surveillance like robots or computers. Cloning is one of the side effects of this conception of the world that presents itself as the best . . . and soon as the only option.

This technological and economic domination is in stark contrast, the author explains, to what he calls "European humanism." This is based on a principle of autonomy of judgment, based specifically on a shared cultural background of history, literature, art and philosophy, all of which are a bad match for techno-libertarianism, obsessed with setting up systems that do not require the slightest subjective judgment: everything is already programmed in advance.

It is, in fact, a serious danger for managers themselves, Sadin tells us. Because if algorithmic guidance is implemented at all levels of the company, with automatic decisions taken remotely, what will managers do in the future? For him, there is no doubt that only those who maintain a certain autonomy of thought will be in a position to play a role, still central today, in the organizations of the future. A call to arms for the thinkers of the future, who will need to offer a more human alternative to the irresistible expansion of digital remote control.

Cost Killing and Cheapness

Raj Patel and Jason Moore, *A History of the World in Seven Cheap Things* (Verso Books, 2017).

Cost killing is a strategy known to all those who have studied management techniques. Cost reduction is a way of improving profitability as if by magic and as such is one of the options often prioritized by organizations seeking to turn around their finances and offer stakeholders a more reassuring image. For economist Raj Patel and historian Jason Moore, this obsession with cost management is the only solution proposed by capitalism, whose nature, one might say, is to "put nature to work at lower cost."

The two authors are interested here in a continuous process of modern history, which they call the "Capitalocene," on the model of the Anthropocene, of course. "We use cheap," they say, "to talk about the process through which capitalism transmutes these undenominated relationships of life, making them into circuits of production and consumption in which these relations come to have as low a price as possible." This strategy has been practiced in many areas: care, work, food, energy, for example. This mode of production has, in fact, seen itself take control of living things without worrying about the consequences, or in any case, postponing the concern for multiple risks until later.

The authors look for those responsible for this situation in the baptismal font of our Modernity: for them, there is no doubt that philosophy is responsible, or rather a philosopher, a French one at that, a certain René Descartes. It was he who, in the first part of the seventeenth century, when merchant ships set out from Holland, his second country, to conquer the world, announced an ontological split between Humans and Nature in these fateful words: "To make ourselves masters and possessors of nature," according to the famous expression of the *Discourse on Method* (1637).

For Patel and Moore, this prescriptive anthropocentrism, a sort of consumerist imperative, enshrines the capitalist method of subjecting Nature to our needs and to its detriment. Cartesian dualism is even presented as "a normative statement on the best way to organise power and hierarchy, Humanity and Nature, Man and Woman, Coloniser and Colonised." This is the very same attitude that made Christopher Columbus the first capitalist, when he was surprised and worried that he couldn't put a price on his discoveries, whether they were new vegetables or new fruits, for example.

But the authors' most persuasive arguments are historical rather than philosophical, as when they point out that the great turning points take place "not when people are starving, but when business as usual no longer works." In other words, it is when the short-term return on investment becomes untenable that the system shows signs of permanent exhaustion. According to the authors, protests against fuel prices—although this book was written before the episode of the Yellow Vests in France at the end of 2018—bear comparisons with the peasants' revolt of 1525.

Unfortunately, Patel and Moore are too quick to conclude this militant book with an "ecology of reparation" based on the values of recognition, redistribution, reimagination, and re-creation, all of which refer to the "troubled history of humanity" that gives the book its subtitle (at least in its French edition).

In reality, in the face of this fear of the future, perhaps it is yet another interpretation of Descartes that can give us some hope. In the expression quoted above, note that the word "as" means precisely that we are not in any way the owners of Nature, and that we should not behave as if we were. Therefore, the word "master" does not refer to the one who exercises dominion but to the one who knows his art; what Descartes advises us instead is precisely to get to know this matter that is Nature to respect it more.

And for that, as he writes a little further on in his *Discourse*, one would have to "try to conquer oneself rather than fortune, and change one's desires rather than the order of the world." In philosophy, as in economics, perhaps the worst form of cheapening is the degradation of language.

Capitalism without Capital, the Main Cause of Social Breakdown?

Jonathan Haskel and Stian Westlake, *Capitalism without Capital. The Rise of the Intangible Economy* (Princeton, NJ: Princeton University Press, 2017).

Do the great economic issues of productivity, inequality, and inflation still have the same meaning in an economy where most investment is intangible? In the material economy, everything is simple: it is enough to measure physical components such as machines or factories. This simplicity does not, however, prevent some of the absurdities pointed out by an economist as important as Samuelson, when he reminds us that "GDP falls when a man marries a cook," or that if you mow your own lawn, you are not engaged in a productive activity. In fact, no official accounts take these productive activities into account, unless, of course, you employ the services of the neighborhood gardener. The same applies to the preparation of family meals if it is done by a home caterer.

But in an immaterial economy, made up of intangible assets such as patents, trademarks, data, artistic creations, designs, and market research, things are no longer quite so simple. And yet, the value chain made up of these assets is on course to become the main source of wealth for the most economically developed nations: intangible investment has been higher than tangible investment in the United States since the mid-1990s. It is following the same direction in Europe, especially in Great Britain, Scandinavia, and to a lesser extent in Germany and France, where the intangible economy is definitively taking over its material counterpart.

For Jonathan Haskel, an economist at Imperial College, and Stian Westlake of the Nesta Foundation, authors of a book devoted to this type of investment, the first challenge is to define it: its cost is irrecoverable, it generates great territorial inequalities, it can be more easily exploited on a large scale, and it is by combining different assets of this kind with each other that the most value can be extracted from it. This is called "innervation," the authors argue, rather than innovation. In the end, intangibles are "scalable and exhibit spillovers": these intangibles can give certain companies such an advantage that they become extraordinarily powerful and destroy all possible local competitors. Inequality, therefore, also concerns companies: those that possess strategic intangible assets, thanks to which the conquest of markets becomes child's play, and then the others.

The problem, however, for our authors is that this transformation is not far from being the cause of all the difficulties, particularly political and social, of our open societies. It creates inequalities not only between companies, of course, but also between people, between countries (particularly in terms of taxation), and between territories: we can see this with the real estate explosion in certain large cities. Above all, they tell us, it generates an inequality of esteem between those who benefit from these evolutions and those who suffer from them, creating a fracture within British society, as we saw at the time of the vote for Brexit, or in France, as witnessed by the emergence of the Yellow Vest movement.

However, for Haskel and Westlake, this change has been too discreet for our politicians to be fully aware of it. Nonetheless, social and special education institutions will have to adapt to this new situation very quickly, by adapting their standards and academic content, otherwise their legitimacy will be undermined.

Those most concerned by these changes could do worse than listen to the podcast masters of scale,[2] created by LinkedIn cofounder Reid Hoffman, which takes this key competence as a starting point for the success stories of American entrepreneurship, based on examples such as Uber, Eventbrite, or Spotify. Contributions include Barry Diller on the need to unlearn, Kevin Systrom of Instagram on how to scale while keeping an idea simple, and Danny Meyer of Shake Shack on how to clarify when an entrepreneur should know how to challenge conventional wisdom.

Why and How to Distinguish between Common Goods

Marie Cornu, Fabienne Orsi, and Judith Rochfeld, *Dictionnaire des biens communs*[3] (PUF, 2017).

What do open-source software, vehicle sharing, or bicycles in successive use (e.g., ex-Gobee bikes) have in common? All of them are a sign of the emergence of profound changes in social practices, giving more room to sharing and collective use. The resurgence of shared assets has been the subject of much work in economics, law, management, and political science, to the point that it is sometimes difficult to know how the notions of collaborative economy, cooperativism, peer-to-peer economy, or public utility activities differ from one another. How do they relate to and drive the thorough transformation of organizations and their management?

It is precisely the objective assigned to this first *Dictionary of Common Goods* to attempt to establish these definitions, distinctions, and important developments in our capitalist-dominated societies.

Let's start with the key word in this book: "common." It is Cicero in his *De officiis* who makes this distinction between private goods and natural goods that belong to all men and whose consumption produces a benefit to each without costing anyone anything. Water is, moreover, designated as the typical example, alongside air, the sea and its coasts, and certain urban spaces, of something which is common by nature, dedicated to the use of all. These resources cannot be appropriated (i.e., no one can claim to own them in any way whatsoever). This transcends all disputes and commercial negotiations, because their value is subordinated to the value of the people who benefit from them. This is why the concept can extend to cultural riches such as language or historical heritage, in the sense of "world heritage . . . of outstanding value to humanity." This is the thesis defended in the work of Elinor Ostrom, winner of the 2009 Nobel Prize in Economics, for her research on the commons.

But speaking positively of the "commons" necessarily brings us into conflict with Garrett Hardin's classic thesis of the "tragedy of the commons,"[4] to which Ostrom's work is partly opposed. According to Hardin's theory, the collective management of resources always leads to their rapid disappearance through overconsumption and depletion. But according to Ostrom, this means ignoring the rules of use that allow a community to manage a "commons," the sharing of negative externalities in a way, more efficiently to preserve this resource. This is, moreover, what Michael Heller and Rebecca Eisenberg's work strongly emphasizes, paradoxically evoking a "tragedy of the anticommons," showing that it is precisely private property, through patent applications, for example, that is an obstacle to innovation.

We discover, entry after entry, that the business world is very directly concerned by these developments. Stakeholders, self-management, mutualism, and the different forms of collective management of an activity are all represented here. Alternative modes of production emerging in recent years, such as productive communities, entrepreneurial coalitions, platform cooperativism (which attempts, in a postcapitalist vein, to allow everyone to be co-owners of the platform they use) also make appearances. This relational logic is described there as "flexible," "affinity-based," "founded on equipotentiality," and finally "contributive," thus relaying the work of the philosopher Bernard Stiegler, which is based on the principle of sharing knowledge between producers and consumers.

But let us not overlook the complexity of these issues, nor their political aspect. Moreover, the notion of the common good, or public good, as the three editors of this collective work point out, has different meanings in the fields of law, economics, philosophy, or management. All of which makes this multidisciplinary approach to the issue all the more valuable, elevating an academic collaboration to the status of public utility.

A Three-Zero Economy with Social Business

Muhammad Yunus, *A World of Three Zeros: The New Economics of Zero Poverty, Zero Unemployment, and Zero Net Carbon Emissions* (Publicaffairs, 2017).

While a former banker who became president of the French Republic is suspected of being the "president of the rich," Muhammad Yunus, nicknamed "the banker of the poor," publishes a book that predicts an economy with three zeros: zero poverty, zero carbon borrowing, and zero unemployment. This is an ambitious program, to say the least, on the part of this rather peculiar capitalist.

Winner of the Nobel Prize in 2006, Yunus is an economist who has successfully developed, notably in Bangladesh, a vast microcredit program centered around the Grameen Bank/Grameen brand, which means "village" in Bengali. Today he is the main global ambassador of what he calls "social business," which is a new way of conceiving the working relationship around the notion of benevolence and above all aims to renew the entrepreneurial logic based on objectives that exclude the payment of dividends. According to Yunus, "300 million poor people throughout the world have been lifted out of extreme poverty" thanks to this system, which allows illiterate and penniless borrowers to start their own business. Moreover, the principle has been extended to rich countries such as the United States. Yunus sees in this result the fact that at Grameen America, the borrower and lender know each other personally, the agreement being the result of face-to-face communication, whereas the credit crisis in 2008 revealed that such contact was lacking in 50 percent of cases. Those contracts had been signed online, without any direct meeting between the parties.

The book, which is sometimes a little repetitive and in places reads like a campaign leaflet, is convincing, particularly on issues relating to extreme poverty. With well-chosen words, Yunus bemoans American bureaucracy, the red tape that prevents many potential actors from taking action: "In Louisiana, a person cannot compose and sell bouquets of more than one variety of flowers in the same vase, without having to pass an exam to obtain a state licence." He rightly returns to the absurdities of the all-too-famous GDP, in which the cost of illiteracy, oppression of women, and racism are not taken into account while the sums spent on armaments and all forms of environmental degradation are precisely calculated.

Finally, Yunus defends the central idea that individual entrepreneurship is the only way out of the impasse in poor countries: he certainly agrees with Thomas Piketty on the nature of the problem, inequality, only to reach a radically different conclusion of how to get out of this impasse, eschewing progressive taxation in favor of offering every individual the opportunity to develop her own activity. And for this, social business invented microcredit.

It should be noted, however, that although he claims not to be an ideologue, Yunus is a utopian, to say the least. When he writes that "we must choose a new system, closer to human nature and its desires," he is merely repeating the discourse that all political parties espouse without exception. When he hopes to make us believe that "the intimate links between good governance, human rights, social justice and economic growth are now widely recognised," he is only looking at a few countries in the world, forgetting a few notable exceptions. Finally, when he points out that infrastructure is important in the long term, he is only repeating what we have known for a long time in countries where, as in France, our 45 percent rate of taxation funds construction projects, roads, hospitals, and schools, which benefit everyone. Nothing very revolutionary about that.

However, social business will be on the agenda in the years to come, because Yunus has convinced the mayor of Paris, Anne Hidalgo, to set up her European center in the Maison des économies sociales et innovantes,[5] recently opened on the banks of the Ourcq canal. According to Yunus himself, there is already talk of hosting there "the first social business Olympics in history." Let's hope that the medal counter will not show triple zero.

Reinventing Ecological Thinking

Timothy Morton, *The Ecological Thought* (Harvard University Press, 2010).

Doing the recycling, giving up meat, using a bicycle instead of a car, voting green—these seem to be the main forms of individual action available to those interested in protecting the planet. But will it be enough? For the philosopher Timothy Morton, a great friend of the singer Björk—who inspired some of his philosophical concepts—and the artist Olafur Eliasson—with whom he has maintained a long dialogue—the answer is clearly negative. Have we entered the age of collapsology? Not for this unusual philosopher, with his rock star airs, who champions a spirit of philosophical and conceptual initiative taking. For Morton, it is a question of nothing less than reinventing the ecological spirit, the ecological society, the ecological conscience by thinking bigger. Because, in his view, "ecological thinking" needs to be big if it is to exist at all. Three strong directions must inform our future actions:

First, we should start from the idea that the world has no center. Nothing and no one is perfectly independent of what happens within or without themselves. We are swimming in an ocean of total interactivity. Morton thus introduces the notion of hyper-object, which has made his reputation on the international philosophical scene: it describes a new way of representing the world based on entities, hyper-objects, which can only be grasped through a set of interactions over which we have little control. They are, in fact, everywhere and nowhere: global warming is one example, or polystyrene, the polymer that is diffused in a contingent—and effectively unquantifiable—manner in many places, such as sandy beaches or the intestines of many animals.

Second, we should stop thinking of tomorrow's world in terms of restrictions. "Capitalist pleasure is not bad because it is too pleasant, but because it is not pleasant enough," Morton writes. It is not a question of praising the system as it is, but of expressing a perspective shift in ecological thinking, moving in a direction that is longer limited to the imbalances of the planet.

Ecological action should finally get rid of the idea of nature, which prevents us from grasping the density of this profound coexistence. The concept of nature makes us think that some things can be considered unnatural, a traditional feature of racist or sexist positions: ecological thinking, on the other hand, teaches us that the "nature" as a background reality has never existed and will never exist again. This is what the Anthropocene is all about: constantly impacted by human activities, flora and fauna are no longer natural, and their continuous transformation has an impact on behavior and human life in general. "The eco-apocalypse always presupposes an audience," explains the author, but in the ecological thinking proposed here, there is neither an audience distinct from supposed nature nor a spectacle independent of who we are ourselves.

In the end, it is to a dark "emancipation with no tomorrow," to a "good without redeeming grace" that Morton invites us, freed from the more worrying forms of environmentalism. But this is precisely where the problem lies: if the author wants to replace anxiety with "love and compassion," he does so in the name of a philosophy that first abolishes the difference between life and nonlife. But then, what kind of love is he talking about when he first abolishes the living world?

If Morton never quite succeeds in expressing this in his book, it is because he seems to imagine a life stripped of its constituent elements, its pathetic and emotional determinations, the capacity for self-experience that we all possess, which makes the world meaningful enough for us to want, if indeed it is still possible, to save it from catastrophe.

What Does Our Rubbish Say about Us?

Baptiste Monsaingeon, *Homo detritus. Critique de la société du déchet*[6] (Seuil, 2017).

It is now estimated that 275 million tons of plastic are dumped into the oceans every year. The trend is only expected to increase, at least until 2100. This is the damning conclusion of an article published in 2015 in *Science*.

Faced with such a bleak prospect, two opposing logics appear to be taking shape: one, stemming from the traditional, growth-oriented model, imagines finding a technological solution to the problem one day; the other, stemming from the so-called circular or zero waste economy, wishes to minimize the use of nonrenewable or nonrecyclable materials, to encourage the dual, reciprocal recognition of the technosphere and the biosphere.

In both cases, says Baptiste Monsaingeon, a researcher at IFRIS,[7] we may be missing the essential question: What does our waste say about us? For the author, these two positions are underpinned by the same ideology, which we inherit from our history. This ideology traces its roots to hygienism, first, pioneered by prefect Eugène Poubelle (the man who gave his name to France's dustbins) who, in the nineteenth century, was among other things the man behind the creation of the sewerage system, and then of political ecology, with the promise of a sustainable world without surplus.

The eco-citizen, a status we all now occupy, more or less, is an "unencumbered self," in the sense of the philosopher Michael Sandel—that is to say, a being who is content to forget her traces, just as she likes to erase her cultural and social origins from her memory. But will this unencumbered individual be able for a long time, with a clear conscience, to continue sorting her waste, while suppressing the knowledge that the gesture is largely symbolic because, for example, half of the plastics produced in the world are never reprocessed? That the gesture is derisory, even if it is not insignificant, compared to the high stakes and the irrevocable nature of certain industrial choices of the past? We are far from certain that we will one day manage to master this way of throwing away without counting the cost.

Monsaingeon's analysis finally sheds light on a completely different perspective. Is there not something in this recurring phenomenon on the scale of humanity that recalls the notion of sovereignty as envisaged by the writer Georges Bataille? Do we not live in excess precisely to assert our power? Is a society that leaves no trace even possible, and, if so, would it be preferable to ours?

Instead, the author suggests that we dig through this heap of rubbish, study our waste to try to understand what it teaches us about ourselves, about our hubris (excess), about our wasteful madness, about our deep-seated penchant for excess. He then engages in some original anthropological reflection, showing that we would know nothing about the Paleolithic if our ancestors had left not trace. He even branches out into rudology, the science concerned with the systematic study of abandoned remains and debris of all kinds.

Monsaingeon's approach is refreshingly original. He does not seek to present our heavenly globe and its power of eternal regeneration as a masterpiece at risk of extinction, instead proposing a new economy of attention toward the world and ourselves, our compulsive behaviors, our frailties. What if the vulnerability of human beings in relation to our planet could inspire new forms of sociability?

The Earth, a New Political Player

Bruno Latour, *Down to Earth; Politics in the New Climatic Regime* (Polity Press, 2019).

Our economic and managerial vocabulary—productivity, growth, rationality, efficiency, and so forth—no longer makes sense because we know that globalization has failed. So says Bruno Latour in one of his latest essays. For the anthropologist and philosopher of science, who is today one of the few French intellectuals whose fame extends beyond Europe, the need to reconsider all our categories is urgent. The Anthropocene obliges us to do so.

If for Donald Trump global warming is for the most part a hoax invented by the Chinese, this opinion seems unfortunately not shared by most mineralogists and geologists. Humans have become a geological force in their own right, so that our ecological conceptions and our political landmarks in general can no longer remain imprisoned in the patterns of the past.

According to the author, this redefinition of our vocabulary must not be undertaken on the grounds of fallacious alternative in which we believe we are caught, either to attach ourselves to a ground or to globalize. This alternative no longer holds. Our soil is giving way, and we will soon be "deprived of Land," like migrants from within, the experience of those, whom we all are, "who feel abandoned by their country." And yet, says Latour,

> There is nothing more innovative, nothing more present, subtle, technical, and artificial (in the positive sense of the word), nothing less rustic and rural, nothing more creative, nothing more contemporary, than to negotiate landing on some ground.

We must, therefore, henceforth seek at all costs a "habitable territory," a new Earth, which can only be apprehended through a redefinition of policy. A right-wing policy? A left-wing policy? This is precisely the kind of contradiction we must get rid of, explains Latour, as well as false conflicts in which we are as if absorbed: local versus global (two utopias that no longer apply), progressivism versus reaction, ecology versus economy, all distinctions that only deny the problem we are facing.

As a way of redefining our categories, the author wonders what name to give to our situation:

> "Earth?" We will think it is the "blue planet." "Nature?" It would be far too vast. "Gaia?" That would be true, but it would take pages and pages to specify its use. "World?" Yes, of course, but there is a risk of mixing with the old forms of globalization. Let us call it, for now, the "Terrestrial," with a capital T to underline the fact that it is a concept.

This revolution in our vocabulary is addressed to everyone, from the leaders of international companies to the thurifers of national identities: the Terrestrial has replaced both the question of globalization and that of crashing back down to earth, this time with a small e.

Latour suggests that it is Europe's responsibility to embark on this path, a continent that has historically been built from below with coal, iron, and steel, but will have to return to ground level again to negotiate a better landing. This new humanism, as the author points out, brings the word "human" back to its etymological root, "humus," the earth, the soil, to which it is related, and from which the word "humility" also originates. A lesson in humility, humus, and humanity that can make one think of the one already contained in Genesis (3:19):

> In the sweat of thy face shalt thou eat bread, till thou return unto the ground; for out of it wast thou taken: for dust thou art, and unto dust shalt thou return.

DATAISM IS NOT A HUMANISM

This section, devoted to the technological changes in the world in general and in organizations in particular, reveals a twofold discontent: first, the spleen of those for whom the world before—before the development of information technology, in particular—was preferable; it was to these that Michel Serres responded in one of his final essays, titled *C'était mieux avant* (Things were better before). And then there is the dissatisfaction of the others, for whom adaptation to the changes in progress can never go fast enough, because happiness always lies over the hill. Such is the general gist of the critique proposed by Barbara Stiegler in *Il faut s'adapter* (We have to adapt). Playing Thumbelina to the experts in the manufacture of consent, such is the alternative we face when weighing advantages or disadvantages of the technological revolution.

It is difficult, in the face of such a debate, not to comment on one of the most widely read books of recent years, *Homo Deus*, which promises to establish for us a "brief history of the future." This text, which does not pretend to be on one side or the other, nevertheless invites us to think about the increasingly obvious separation between intelligence (algorithmic) and conscience (moral). It shares this aim with a whole series of essays devoted to examining the relationship we have with our machines, questioning the artificial character of their intelligence. While the sociologist Dominique Cardon is interested in "our lives in the age of big data," the urologist and entrepreneur Laurent Alexandre urges us to adapt ourselves to what he calls the "war of intelligences," as if this conflict were inevitable. The philosopher Eric Sadin, who we meet again here, seems much less optimistic when he tells us that we will soon be subjected to a universal panopticon in all areas of our lives, both professional (data-driven management) and personal (see on this subject the analysis of the "attention market" by Bruno Patino). He calls for all forms of resistance that would allow us to counter the announced algorithmic bio-hygienism.

Working toward this goal, philosopher Maurizio Ferraris advises us to learn to let go of our smartphones for a while because they are a major contributor to the new balance of power taking shape between our machines and us. Finally, he appeals to us to remain vigilant as to the quality of our cultural consumption in an effort that can be compared to that of Alexis Grinbaum, who wonders about the violence of robots. And their mischievous use: in this respect we would do well to heed the words of Luc de Brabandère, who reminds us of the need to preserve our quite precious (human) abilities to think and to evaluate.

Faced with the challenges of the present moment and of a future variously prophesied, I conclude by discussing the work of the sociologist Antonio Cassili, who points out the double inadequacy of artificial intelligence: on the one hand, by failing to do what we thought it was capable of doing (it was supposed to relieve us of work that could be automated, whereas, in fact, it only seems to add to it); and on the other hand, by showing itself incapable, despite the promises of many zealots of the new technologies, of giving meaning to work.

Against Nostalgia

Michel Serres, *C'était mieux avant*[8] (Le Pommier, 2017).

"'It was better before,' say the pensioners, whose expenses *Thumbelina* will be covering for a long time." With this provocative sentence, which also provides the title for one of Michel Serres's final works, the philosopher reminds us that it is deeply mistaken and naive to assume that our era is worse than the previous one. *Thumbelina*, of course, was the name the philosopher gave to a previous work, published in 2012, in which he described the world to come, not his own, but that of algorithmic thinking and the end of the knowledge era.

Michel Serres, therefore, has no wish to join people of his own age who consider that today is worse than yesterday. In a series of striking examples taken from a life that lasted almost nine decades, the philosopher does his bit for the health of the nation by reminding us of two or three facts that we really should know.

First, the Thumbelina generation has made progress in terms of gender equality. "As a widow, Marie Curie, so brilliant in physics and chemistry that she won two Nobel prizes, had to endure a painful ordeal because some newspapers accused her of having a lover; I don't remember the male being targeted; our memories as macho men forget this unjust pain." And lest we forget, not so long ago, sex education simply did not exist: "Below the belt," he writes, "was terra incognita."

Second, the generation represented by Serres's *Thumbelina* has made extraordinary progress in the medical field. Serres remembers the time in his youth when the question of paternity and maternity had to be asked in these terms: How many children would have to be born for two or three to survive? This progress has extended into the everyday comforts of life, down to such prosaic details as the wearing of new shoes. He explains it in the following terms:

> Our shoes, before, their hard leather used to hurt your heels and ankles. To soften these shoes, we had to walk for weeks during which our toes sprouted blisters, corns and calluses. The rich, it was said, used to make their valets wear their shoes for two months so that they could break them in.

Third, Serres reminds us of a point in history that we tend to forget in our media-saturated age—namely, the power of rumor in ancient times. "I don't know anyone who has ever really heard the famous de Gaulle[9] broadcast of 18 June," he writes. "Both sides flooded the radio broadcasts of the adversary with parasites. Any message reached us scrambled." From this point of view, and despite the many imperfections of our media system, we can indeed accept the idea that some progress has been made in the past fifty years.

The academician finally suggests that flow has now triumphed over stock, and that this is excellent news, that our institutions are to be reinvented, that the possibilities of coding are such as to overwhelm all thought, and that all this has been written since Pascal and Leibniz developed the calculating machine.

But on each of these points, it must be acknowledged that everything remains largely to be reinvented and that Serres leaves his Thumbelina all alone in the face of the demiurgic task. Will it succeed in reinventing itself in the face of developments in artificial intelligence? Nothing is less certain. She will no doubt have to rely on what Pascal called the spirit of finesse. Indeed, it is very likely that soon interpreting, decoding, and contrasting situations and contexts will be more important than mumbling a few clichés from computer language. And let us bet that schools and universities, here as elsewhere, will play a central role.

A Reminder That Economics and Biology Are Not One and the Same

Barbara Stiegler, "Il faut s'adapter". Sur un nouvel impératif politique[10] **Gallimard, "Nrf Essais" (2019).**

If one common refrain appears to unite all newspapers in the Western world, irrespective of political sensitivity or geographical context, it would probably be "backwardness." Take France, for instance. In terms of the fight against cardiovascular and psychiatric diseases, medicinal cannabis, outpatient surgery, fish farming, digitalization of SMEs, energy renovation of buildings, or support for job seekers, France is, the newspapers regularly remind us, "behind the times." We are well accustomed to being told that we, collectively, have got it wrong, leaving us to watch in silence as history unfolds before our eyes.

"Trapped in the backwaters," spectators to "the boundless advances in the performance of our species": such is Barbara Stiegler's summary of the situation. She alludes to a discourse that extends far beyond the realm of journalism and can be detected more or less explicitly in the majority of political campaigns, as well as in the positions adopted by many business leaders. Drawing on her background in political philosophy, Stiegler evokes the innumerable "injunctions to adapt, . . . to increase the pace, to abandon our immobility and stave off the spectre of deceleration . . . disparaging all forms of stasis in the name of the flow."

By making this background noise the characteristic feature, and the leitmotiv of neoliberalism, Stiegler argues that the latter is not as hung up on the notion of homo œconomicus as we tend to assume but is more concerned with a particular conception of human evolution and the way in which living things are transformed. This biological anchoring of neoliberalism is illustrated by the life and work of Walter Lippmann, an American journalist who died in 1974. For this political adviser and great polemist, the responsibility of the "ruling classes" resided in the "manufacture of consent," a concept that Noam Chomsky subsequently tore to pieces.

This guiding idea led Lippmann to subjugate the human and social sciences entirely to his ultimate objective, a form of pragmatism buoyed by an unwavering faith in the competence of "experts." Because citizens are not omniscient and are, in fact, unable to grasp the complexity of the world, it seems only obvious that a government of specialists could provide effective answers to the antagonistic desires of the mob. Only the leader, capable of "revising his stereotypes," seemed able to maintain a hierarchical distance from the constituent elements of the people, that mass of apathetic and capricious individuals always lagging behind the pace of scientific and technical knowledge change.

What can we say about this analysis that, the author astutely notes, has exerted a considerable formative influence on America's economic elites? Another American philosopher, John Dewey, refuted Lippmann's theses and argued that primarily "the public and its problems" were at the root of democracy, rather than consultants and leaders. He noted that flexibility, so coveted nowadays, has always had two possible meanings: servitude, or the ability to learn from experience to decide for oneself what is appropriate; or to defer, or to anticipate.

Being late is precisely the option preferred by Socrates, arriving just as Gorgias, a sophist who teaches the art of persuasion, finishes his speech. Everyone is surprised by this lack of respect for propriety. But Socrates has not come to hear a speech; he has come to dialogue with his interlocutors. His gesture of adjournment is only a way of making his contemporaries understand that what he wants, with this strategic and deliberate delay, is to oppose the univocal character of the presentation, its unfolding without surprise. Socrates scrambles temporality to resist once again the small truths that are too quickly stated. And reveals that reflection always requires a step to the side, thus reminding us that life cannot be reduced to a contest of speed.

Human Consciousness Challenged by Data

Yuval Noah Harari, *Homo Deus. A Brief History of Tomorrow* (Penguin Random House, 2017).

We have known for more than a century that, at least physically, machines have supplanted humans. This is to be welcomed, of course: when it comes to engineering work or freight transport, for example, this is a considerable advance for all mankind. But according to Yuval Noah Harari, the Israeli academic whose first important book, *Homo sapiens*, had a planetary impact, the issue we now face is the overtaking of humans on a cognitive level, as if it were the latest avatar of the cybernetic revolution, with consequences that could be very profound. A famous study by Oxford researchers Frey and Osborne predicts that 99 percent of insurance agents and telemarketers will have lost their jobs by 2033, as well as 98 percent of sports referees, 97 percent of cashiers, and 91 percent of tour guides. The difficulty that awaits us at the turn of the 2030s will be to create jobs that are not immediately replaced by artificial intelligence. And for Harari, this will not be a piece of cake.

In this second work, just as striking as the first, Harari sets out to describe and illustrate the irresistible transformation of Homo sapiens into *Homo Deus*, like upgrading to the new version of a software program. There are many reasons why this evolution is inevitable. Here are two of them.

First, medical research is progressing and is aimed at finding solutions for health problems; but at the same time, it is increasing human capacity: medicines that treat memory impairment in the elderly can just as easily boost the memory capacities of younger people. This is the Viagra syndrome, so to speak: designed by Pfizer laboratories to help men suffering from erectile dysfunction, it rapidly became a (excellent from what I've heard) tool for increasing sexual performance.

Second, artificial intelligence is progressing more rapidly than we realize. A recent study of 86,220 volunteer Facebook users found that if you have used the "like" button more than three hundred times, the algorithm can predict your opinions and desires better than your relatives. When we offer our data to large American companies in return for messaging services and comic videos of dogs and cats, we look like (to borrow the author's unfortunately accurate simile) the natives who surrendered whole islands and territories as big as countries to the European conquistadors in return for a few colorful beads.

No, dataism is not humanism. The mutation of Homo sapiens into Homo Deus will not take place without some minor damage. So, it is difficult to predict what will become of managers in a few years' time. Will they, in turn, be "Uberized"? One wonders what use we really have for managers, now that the algorithm developed by this company is capable of supervising drivers. In a striking passage, Harari cites the example of a Hong Kong-based company that recently appointed Vital to its board of directors, an algorithm that, like the other members, gives its opinion on the possible investments of this firm, based on the compilation of mountains of data that none of the other board members have the capacity to analyze in such detail. Harari plays this anecdote for laughs, but one can well imagine, indeed, that in the near future this algorithm might become an excellent investor, make a fortune, and acquire a real estate portfolio that it could then let in return for a comfortable income. And if the tenants don't pay the rent on time, the algorithm could probably hire a lawyer to take them to court. We might thus find ourselves with very rich algorithms that own most of the planet, alongside other nonhuman entities such as states and corporations, and very poor managers.

This book, whose worldwide success is not unwarranted, raises a whole series of questions that our generation will have to answer. Because, for the first time in history, intelligence and consciousness seem to have definitively parted ways. How important will consciousness be compared to the intelligence of machines? And what fundamentally human intelligence can stand up to the rise of AI? Soon, very soon perhaps, we will have to decide.

The Power of Algorithms, the Rebirth of Criticism?

Dominique Cardon, A quoi rêvent nos algorithmes? Nos vies à l'heure des big data[11] (Seuil, "La république des idées", 2015).

The development of algorithms is too serious and too important a matter to be left to scientists alone. Such is the core argument of Dominique Cardon's essay, an attempt to get to the root of what is really going on in the calculating society that, whether we like it or not, is our reality. Cardon's objective with this tome is to help nonspecialists gain some understanding of how modern computers qualify, integrate, and sort the data circulating on the Web, including the 144 billion emails exchanged every day by three billion internet users. What do these countless calculations tell us about the world?

To enable us to better understand, he proposes an original interpretative approach based on four key notions:

- popularity (measured using tools such as Google Analytics),
- authority (the order of Google search results being the most familiar example),
- reputation (thanks, for example, to the number of friends that an individual or a brand has on Facebook)
- and, finally, prediction: Amazon is well known for proposing books based on previous readings of those who are "similar to us."

The author highlights several inescapable phenomena, such as the fact that it is no longer expertise that prevails but the "wisdom of the crowds": when it comes to information, for example, it is no longer the journalist's judgment that prevails, in choosing subjects, but that of the users, according to the number of times information is shared.

However, this behaviorism is not without its critics and weak points: authority measured by popularity alone, filter effect—users can no longer escape from their bubbles because the choices offered to them are based only on their previous choices—and, even more seriously, the complete disappearance of human discernment. In fact, these calculations bet on the fact that individuals always share the opinions of their friends and that their future is entirely a product of their past. Algorithms are thus incapable of imagining that human beings, unlike machines, are capable of branching off, of showing skill or even moral sensitivity. They cannot conceive that a society can sometimes break out of the hierarchies that haunt it. Like spies constantly on their guard, like a cash register on high alert, they are only interested in the quantifiable traces of our behavior and in archiving them; in other words, keeping a running tab of our past behavior.

Are we, therefore, condemned, in the author's words, to become "little mechanical mice in the claws of computers"? Or should we rather, in the face of this deluge of data, as Silicon Valley guru Chris Anderson has argued, seize the opportunity to definitively replace the complexity of the human sciences, such as sociology or anthropology, with the limpidity of mathematical calculations?

Caught between these two sides of the same coin, I am inclined to join Cardon on the third path that he proposes in this book: faced with the power of algorithms, it is important not to surrender our faculty of judgment and to exercise our critical capacities while we are still capable of doing so.

Human Intelligence versus Artificial Intelligence

Laurent Alexandre, *La Guerre des intelligences*[12] (Jean-Claude Lattès, 2017).

In May 2017, Alpha Go inflicted a 3–0 thrashing on Ke Jie, the undisputed world champion of the game of Go. This new triumph of artificial intelligence was a much more considerable shock than the one caused by the victory, not without a certain degree of controversy, of Deep Blue over Kasparov ten years previously. The game of Go is supposed to be entirely intuitive, meaning that mere statistical mastery of all the game's possibilities cannot guarantee victory.

For Laurent Alexandre, whose media appearances in recent years have made him a standard bearer for the risks posed by artificial intelligence, we have entered a cycle of rapid progression of AI in all fields, including medicine, commerce, and public affairs administration. A surgeon and urologist with a degree in political science and business management, and an entrepreneur since cofounding the website Doctissimo, he is particularly well-placed to apprehend from all angles the opportunities and risks offered by the world that the high priests of AI, led by Zuckerberg and Bezos, have in store for us.

The book is devoted to a sort of risk analysis: biological intelligence on the one hand, AI on the other. For the essayist, the melding of IT and human resources management is nearly upon us, because silicon brains and biological brains will soon have to merge. The rise of AI, and its hybridization with our own existence, have only just begun. Ray Kurzweil, Google's director of engineering, is in no doubt about it: by 2045, we will have a supersonic AI a billion times more powerful than all our human brains combined. Moreover, we will soon no longer be able to do without this new form of intelligence:

"soon, only the capacities for mathematical analysis offered by AI will be able to certify that it is indeed the President herself who has declared war," Alexandre predicts, reminding us that even the certification of reality will eventually be a matter for AI.

For Alexandre, the main problem is the gap between the increase in neuroplasticity of the happy few who will be able to access these developments and the reduction of this same neuroplasticity in those who will not have access to them, due to the "externalization" of their talents and reasoning capacities. For example, the memory skills of London taxi drivers have been in freefall since they started using Waze, the mobile GPS navigation application.

We have every reason to be afraid: if Facebook will soon be able to read our thoughts and anticipate our every impulse, we will never again be able to even glimpse what Facebook does to our heads, how Facebook thinks about us and thinks for us, as the complexity of its algorithm continues to increase. And if e-services become perfectly attuned to our deepest aspirations and desires, the author asks this crucial question: What will be the point of "engaging in tedious and intimidating social relationships" in the near future?

Alexandre is less persuasive when he reveals the limitations of his definition of intelligence, something akin to IQ. More convincing is his analysis of the democratic and economic conditions that determine our capacity for participation in what he calls, ironically perhaps, the great "digital feast." Laurent Alexandre opposes both anti-silicon prejudice and the concept of universal income, which he sees as a form of resignation that shirks the need to engage with the "complementarity quotient" represented by AI. At the very least, he proposes scenarios that are worthy of discussion.

What future do we want, and above all what limits do we give to the transformation of our humanity on the three points that fundamentally define it: the integrity of our physical body, our individual subjectivity, and finally, the right not to know everything about our future? To answer these questions, the author warns, we will need at least to show courage and no doubt wisdom as well.

Is My "n+1" a Replicant?

Markus Gabriel, *The Meaning of Thought* (Polity, 2021).

Let us imagine for a moment that we are only animated beings, programmed by computers belonging to a society far more advanced than ours. As in *Westworld*, the HBO series, the world would be nothing more than an amusement park, full of androids like us, for the entertainment of computers and other calculators whose reasons would be beyond our comprehension.

Such is the thought experiment proposed by German philosopher Markus Gabriel in this essay: an experiment that we have little reason to mock, because even a Nobel Prize winner in physics, the American astrophysicist and cosmologist George Fitzgerald Smoot, considers it conceivable.

However, there is, according to the author, no need to resort to such elaborate scenarios; artificial intelligence, weak or strong, remains and will remain for all eternity an artifact, a creation of human intelligence. Yet for this philosopher, who rose to prominence as the youngest holder of a chair of philosophy in Germany in 2009, human intelligence is not only capable of proposing solutions to the sort of abstract problems that could just as well be solved by a computer program. It also knows how to ask questions that relate to our very existence, concrete, existential questions that do not concern our machines. In short, he explains, "we don't know how to build machines that are more intelligent than the rules we have set for them." It's as if, to use the author's Houellebecqian expression, "AI is to HI (human intelligence) as the map is to the territory." Machines are guided only by more or less elaborate calculation procedures and thus have no real autonomy. In other words, they are incapable of dictating their own terms of engagement.

And Gabriel also observes that, even if it is the work of the philosopher Frege that made the digital mutation possible, through the logical revolution it engendered, we must not lose sight of the words of another philosopher, Ludwig Wittgenstein, who reminds us that the phrase "I may be dreaming" makes absolutely no sense. For if I am indeed dreaming, then the words I use no longer have the same meaning as those I use in everyday life. And in this case, these words no longer have the same meaning at all as the ones that we are supposed to give them in the flow of conscious life.

Should we therefore stop worrying for no reason, stop wondering, for example, whether the boss and the new trainee are "replicants"? Instead, we should perhaps concern ourselves with what is true and what is not, starting with the ongoing ethical problems thrown up by the workings of our machines. "Computers don't solve our moral problems, they tend to make them worse," says Gabriel, "because to make smartphones we exploit rare earths in poor countries, and to maintain our digital reality we use plastic for our hardware and waste incredible amounts of energy." He adds that the software solutions developed on the western fringes of the United States, which are presented as metaphysically neutral, are in fact driven by a libertarian value system with a strong transhumanist undertone.

It is also entirely legitimate, the author suggests, to worry about what he calls the "collateral damage of digitization," such as endemic piracy, attention deficit disorders among the young, widespread social surveillance in China, or the "link farms" that allow clients to build an artificial fanbase on the internet.

In the end, it is not so much the revenge of the androids of *Westworld* that we should be concerned with but, rather, "regaining the sense of thought," in the words of the "new realism" that Gabriel champions in philosophy. This can only be achieved through our biological sensory system, in particular our ability to feel ourselves, a sense of self-affection to which our machines are completely insensitive.

Can Our Lives Escape the Power of Algorithms?

Éric Sadin, La Vie algorithmique. Critique de la raison numérique[13] (L'Échappée, 2015).

Have we finally found, with algorithms and their invisible proliferation, the best way to govern our behavior? What is really so wrong with systems that take care of our future demands and continuously inform us about our heartbeat, as well as the state of road traffic, the state of stocks in our favorite shops, or the automatic regulation of the bath temperature according to our stress level of the day? Rather than having a law to respect or a boss to obey, isn't it more satisfying to have above you only software that has been designed to ensure that it constantly provides us with personalized advice, which is refined according to our past choices, without us having to make the slightest effort at any time?

In this new essay, Éric Sadin seems to have strong doubts about this, even when he describes the evening comforts of an average individual benefiting from such advantages:

> You get into bed: the intuitive mattress detects lumbar tension and starts an appropriate massage, which gradually helps you to fall asleep. The automated home management system receives the information that you have fallen asleep, initiates the nightly air purification process and wishes you goodnight in a subdued and subliminal voice: "May this night be sweet and bring you healthy rest."

But Sadin is much more sanguine when it comes to understanding the great stakes of algorithmic optimization and the implantation of sensors in objects, as well as living beings. For this writer, one of the rare contemporary thinkers to take a direct interest in this major paradigmatic change, this total surrender of ourselves and our aspirations to the robots is cause for concern. For what is to be put in place is equivalent to a system of absolute rationalization, a universal panopticon that allows us to steer our lives, as well as our organizations, with a level of mathematical theorizing unexplored until now. We can surmise as much from the words of a former Google boss, who not so long ago explained that "the power of individual targeting through technology will be so perfect that it will be very hard for people to see or consume something that has not been tailored to them."

This surrender of ourselves and our desires has a despotic quality, making it impossible to express a desire that has not already been short-circuited by algorithmic prediction. This new instrumental rationality seems to want to shirk from what is nevertheless resistant, our human sensitivity, our affective subjectivity, the force that allows us to create, to say no, to deviate from our predetermined path, to avoid disaster. This is, moreover, in a typical example, what Robert McNamara, secretary of defense under Kennedy and Johnson, belatedly recognized: the war in Vietnam was launched based on figures, and the United States neglected to assess the situation using other criteria such as history, language, the values of Southeast Asia, and so forth.

There is a lesson to be learned here for many professions, such as management, that involve decision making. The world must also be measured qualitatively. Data-driven management is a temptation that will be difficult to resist, but it will be necessary to do so if we want to preserve the imaginative capacities of organizations. Only the human sciences and their singular virtues are capable of opposing the totalitarian project of algorithmic "bio-hygienism." Among those who are perhaps more aware of this than others, engineers themselves, and especially the signatories of the critical engineering manifesto,[14] when they recall how, now more than ever before, computer science needs input from architecture, philosophy, and the history of art.

From Attention to Capture

Bruno Patino, La Civilisation du poisson rouge. Petit traité sur le marché de l'attention[15] (Grasset, 2019).

Oh, bygone days, time when the former boss of TF1[16] announced that his channel was selling "available human brain time" to Coca-Cola, assuming that this was his job. And yet, despite the scandal these remarks caused in France at the time, there is precious little to suggest that his vision of the "attention economy" was mistaken, a world in which viewers are cognitive prey for the big consumer brands.

Since then, this rule of the game seems to have been intensified and even radicalized by the action of influential digital players. To the extent that the time we spend staring at screens to check our messages, count our "friends" on Facebook, and upload photos to Instagram represents a subject of concern of which we, parents, employers, or simple internet users are more and more conscious . . . or less and less unconscious.

Parents and employers may draw some consolation from the fact that the human sciences are beginning to coin terms for these thoroughly modern problems:

- nomophobia—no mobile phone phobia—when we are anxious to know we are suddenly far from our phone;
- athazagoraphobia, the anxiety experienced by millennials when their posts don't generate enough "likes";
- or phnubbing, which consists of staring at your iPhone while others, perhaps your girlfriend or your colleagues, are talking to you. It is almost as if, by consulting our screens several hundred times a day, our nerves and impulses are allowed to permanently override our capacity for judgment.

Does this awareness change our habits? Not at all, because we are precisely incapable of doing so. This is what Bruno Patino tells us in essence, pointing out that it is now possible to compare our attention span, which would be about nine seconds, with that of a fish in a jar, which we estimate to be one second less, the period of time from which "it resets its mental universe to zero."

For Patino, a top manager in the media sector but also a connoisseur of the California development models that gave rise to the GAFAMs, which he has been observing for at least two decades, this result owes nothing to chance. It is the consequence of the transformation of attention into capture, due to the development of neuroscientific research carried out within the Persuasive Technology Lab at Stanford University, which has made captology its hobbyhorse.

Captology is the science of addiction. If we look at our mobile phones like machines, automatically, we do not do it by an effort of will but by addiction—that is to say, without really consenting to it. As Bernard Stiegler, who Patino quotes here, rightly points out, "Disruption moves faster than will."

In the very last part of this essay, however, the author tries to reassure and console us by evoking the possibilities of future emancipation. He remains as optimistic as he was when he first encountered the utopian possibilities of the Web, while unfortunately giving us all the reasons to be even more afraid of them. Indeed, he evokes, which is very worrying, the phenomenon of inversion that occurs when the content published on the Web coming from robots or fake accounts becomes more abundant than that produced by the real audience, to the point that soon our behavior as users will be considered as deviating from the norm, that of computers.

All of which leaves us with precious little hope, with even the metaphorical goldfish falling prey to pessimism: recent scientific studies have shown that goldfish can suffer from severe depression when kept in bowl that inhibits their growth. But the human being is not an aquarium animal, and it may not be too late to toss it back into the outdoor pond, its natural environment.

The author's reminder of the Rule of St. Benedict, "one third for the body, the second for work and the third for intellectual life or prayer," is enlightening from this point of view. Flanked on all sides by screens, but with the days still just twenty-four hours long, we will necessarily have to set aside time and space for other activities.

Under pressure from the captologists, our response may or may not be one of real existential significance.

Smartphone Addiction Alert

Maurizio Ferraris, *Total Mobilisation* (PUF, 2017).

Are we still able to disconnect? To turn off the mobile phone that wakes us up at night, that can ring at any time of the day, entreating us to pick up, constantly demanding our attention? What can we do in the face of this "total mobilization" that qualifies in every respect the relationship of dependence that we have with our smartphones?

For Maurizio Ferraris, our attention-grabbing mobile phones are first and foremost small order-receiving machines. Thanks to them, we have imperceptibly entered the reign of absolute availability, where we can by summoned at any time. Why do we feel obliged to answer? Could it be the link that unites us to our correspondents and makes us tend toward a "hyper-responsibility" toward those who call us? There is more to it than that, the author assures us: what obliges us to respond is, first and foremost, the regime of documentality that these small, high-tech objects establish. These, let us not forget, remain above all spaces that allow us to record facts, to memorize documents of all kinds at any moment of the day. In other words, these seemingly docile and inoffensive machines are, in fact, establishing a new regime of power. And, as Ferraris explains very well, there can be no power without record keeping.

So, what is to be done? Is there still time to escape the grasp of this soft power that records our actions, our movements as well as our purchases? Are our smartphones taking us away from civilization, despite the fact that so many of us—50 percent of the world's population, all the same—consider them to be vital tools for our mobility and independence? In the last third of the book, after having warned against a generalized surveillance society, Ferraris finally reveals himself to be much more optimistic than he at first led us to believe:

> Our structural dependence is also a cultural opening, and it is certain that today, much more so than in the days of the mass media, culture is accessible to an extraordinarily large number of people. . . . For the first time, humanity has an infinite library of books, films and music at its disposal.

Ultimately, this essay can be read as a citizen's warning about the use we make of our everyday correspondence tools. As such, it seems important to maintain, both ethically and legally, a certain degree of control over our digital traces. This book also presents a bold argument for coming to grips with these connected, ever-watchful objects and using them to reinvent the cultural resources available on digital networks: here the responsibility of new media publishers appears as central.

Indeed, it is up to media and cultural companies, particularly in Europe, to mobilize as much as possible to seize the historic opportunity for didactic and educational openness presented by these powerful tools of mass attention.

Faced with the "Black Swan," Do We Code or Do We Philosophize?

Luc de Brabandère, *Homo informatix* (Le Pommier, 2017).

An engineer, a mathematician, a logician, and a philosopher are traveling together on a road in Scotland. Perched on a rock, a black sheep watches them go by.

> As you can see, says the engineer, in Scotland the sheep are black.
>
> You probably meant to say that some Scottish sheep are black, the mathematician replies.
>
> Let's not get carried away, adds the logician, all we can say is that there is at least one black sheep in Scotland!
>
> And yet, the only thing we can be really sure of, the philosopher concludes, is that it is black on this side.

With this short fable, Luc de Brabandère plunges us straight into the heart of the procedural thinking typical of the algorithmic era. Homo informatix takes its place among the essays that for some time now have been trying to think about computer science with a view to prospective and long-term analysis. Nothing unusual for this former partner of the Boston Consulting Group, who now presents himself as a "corporate philosopher." Further, the author's engineering training does not push him, to say the least, to accept too quickly the hegemonic pretensions of the algorithmic society, often presented as the inescapable horizon of our age.

In a series of insightful reflections, the author recalls truths that we tend to forget too quickly. Social networks provide an arena in which hatred of all kinds and malevolence toward others can be expressed without nuance. The internet is not free: Brabandère challenges the image of "surfing" to talk about traffic; if there is surfing, it is to better underline the risk of being finally swallowed up by a wave too high for us. And last but not least, the internet comes at a price: "Data is not given," he reminds us, "it is taken from you."

It is, therefore, high time to formulate a "critique of automatic reason." The author does so by showing that the promises of big data cannot be kept, for at least two reasons: first, their inability to identify "black swans" (i.e., accidents, the unexpected things we cannot predict); second, their impoverished definition of intelligence, a logical-mathematical capacity that counts and ranks but does not take our emotional faculties into account.

In the end, data analysis always fails to reveal the essential. Certainly, one advantage of computers is that they can handle some of the necessities of daily life, but they will never be capable of desire on our behalf:

> A computer can recognise a face, but it cannot find it beautiful. A computer has memory, but it cannot have remembrances. It can produce images, but it has no imagination. A computer can learn from its mistakes, but it cannot regret them, it can compare ideas, but it cannot have them.

Underneath the flood of data put into circulation, the question of their interpretation and the meaning we give them thus arises. These data can never replace our judgment, otherwise we would run the risk, as Brabandère reminds us, of taking seriously Coluche's joke "that advised sick people not to go to hospital. Because, he said, the probability of dying in a hospital bed is ten times higher than the probability of dying in your own bed at home."

In the face of developments in artificial intelligence, the advice he gives to Homo informatix is not to rush into coding but to philosophize without delay. For it is not the prospect of an artificial intelligence capable of instituting its own intentionality that we should fear but, rather, our inability to ask ourselves, in our schools, our companies, and our laboratories, the fundamental questions of the ethical and political scope that we attach to our actions, not that they have been transformed by the perfection of machines.

Down with IQ! Long Live the Blue Brain?

Catherine Malabou, *From IQ Measurement to Artificial Brains*, translated by Carolyn Shread (New York: Columbia University Press, 2019).

The verdict of the world best-seller *Homo Deus* is very clear: in the economic and political world to come, consciousness will be optional, whereas intelligence will become compulsory. After all, intelligence is becoming more and more important to us every day.

But the question of what it really means is not the least of the concerns to which Yuval Noah Harari's somewhat peremptory statement invites us.

Throughout the twentieth century, this question has been asked without ever really finding a satisfactory answer; the "intelligence gene" is nowhere to be found, and IQ score is an attempt to quantify something they can never quite grasp. As for philosophers, from Bergson onward, the deeper they delve into the problem, the more it is human stupidity that they end up investigating, as Jacques Derrida did in his last seminar in 2003, *The Beast and the Sovereign*.

Among contemporary philosophers, however, none better than Catherine Malabou, who, incidentally, wrote her thesis under the guidance of Derrida, has attempted to understand how our scientific knowledge of the brain informs our possibilities of knowing what "intelligence" means. In her view, the biological and the symbolic must be combined, and the brain is the seat of intelligence because of its "natural plasticity." This observation leads her to two important considerations.

The first is to make the link here between the plasticity of the brain and an epigenetic approach to intelligence, drawing upon the scientific tools used to study the adaptation of genes to the environment, without modifying our DNA. Gone are the days of genetic determinism, this is the age of neuronal plasticity: our body and our brain constantly respond to their environment and transform themselves accordingly without having to rectify the genome. In this "biology of interaction," it is no longer the innate that is the source of acquired knowledge but, rather, acquired knowledge that continuously influences the innate.

The second major idea leads the author to question the frontier she previously imagined between human intelligence and the "artificial plasticity" of computers. As the "Blue Brain" project, which aims to build a synthetic brain based on the architectural model of the human brain, tends to show, it is quite possible that we will soon have to abandon the distinction between the two. In the age of the learning machine, based on the capacity of machines to learn from their mistakes and thus gain independence, the epigenetic revolution of artificial intelligence is on the horizon.

This book opens fascinating perspectives, two of which stand out in particular. First, the relationship between humans and machines will undergo profound changes. Soon, our electronic devices will adapt to who we are. Smartphones are already doing this, and some of them will only work if they can see your face. In Spike Jonze's film *Her*, Joaquin Phoenix's character is so attached to Samantha, a revolutionary operating system, because she is a perfect simulation of the ideal lover who, anticipating her slightest desires, knows him better than he knows himself.

If we are presented with two works of art, for example Edgar Degas's *Les chevaux de course à Longchamp* and an impeccable copy, one being the perfect replica of the other to the point that it is impossible to differentiate one from the other, what difference does it make that one is original and the other a copy? Probably none. And as our author notes, this point is all the more disturbing because we are the first to simulate our emotions in everyday life. In other words, it is not the way the robots work that is changing us, because we already behave like them.

This is undoubtedly the secret of intelligence: its eternal potential for metamorphosis. As the author reminds us in her conclusion, it was the sages of ancient Greece who, better than anyone else, perceived the power of intelligence in the form of the mètis: a faculty of adaptation constantly reiterated in the face of the vicissitudes of existence; an ability to play on the unforeseen, a ruse consisting of skilfully mocking ordinary thought procedures.

The "AI Punchers," or the Economics of Micro-Tasking

Antonio Cassili, En attendant les robots. Enquête sur le travail du clic[17] **(Seuil, 2019).**

We generally think that digital work is outsourced to machines and that this is its main characteristic. In this we are mistaken, because in whole regions of the Philippines, Mozambique, and Uganda, to name but a few, people are hard at work doing what artificial intelligence is supposed to do but is not able to do. You only need look at Amazon Mechanical Turk, the service that Amazon launched in 2005, to see for yourself. It recruits "click workers" from all over the world to perform micro-tasks such as identifying and classifying sounds and images, renaming files, querying dedicated sites, or producing short comments. In the ever-growing data economy, the value of a Facebook like can be anywhere between $0.0005 and $174, whereas the value of a tweet is between $0.001 and $560.

These "AI punchers," to use the neat expression coined by the sociologist Antonio Cassili, are the "billions of little hands that, day after day, activate the puppet of weak automation." This phenomenon stems from the concomitant emergence of global platforms and the gig economy, and our sociologist chooses to qualify it as digital labor. Labor, to signify a workforce that cannot be assimilated to a salaried job (in this case, the word work would be a better fit); digital, because it is indeed a job that the finger does, by transforming masses of information with low added value into data that can be traded on world markets.

This revealing and well-documented book contradicts at least two widely held assumptions about the future of work: on the one hand, its end as predicted by Jeremy Rifkin, which appears to be a subjective hypothesis; on the other hand, the myth of total automation, which seems to be unattainable. The fuel for these data processing systems is provided by the precarious clickers of the southern hemisphere, certainly, but also by the "producers," users of Facebook or Instagram. The same will soon be true of so-called autonomous or self-driving cars, which will still require a "vehicle operator" (i.e., a driver).

This research, heir to the Italian workerism (operaismo) tradition, serves to lift the veil on the immensity of the fake market that is fed by the semisecret activity of "click farms." These farms, responsible for optimizing the number of followers of a brand, or simply maintaining the buzz, represent a huge market. According to the author, it was already estimated that in 2013, "the sale of fake followers on Twitter represented a turnover of 360 million dollars per year, while on Facebook, fake clicks are estimated to have generated 200 million." Also, in a series of pages that are particularly striking for Uber users, it is easier to understand why almost two-thirds of a driver's day is spent updating his profile, maintaining customer relations, selecting the right fares, and skilfully refusing others, attempting to limit dead miles. Cassili also describes some of the strategies of "reverse engineering of the platform" that drivers employe.

Two main schools of thought emerge regarding this micro-tasking economy taking shape on the horizon. The first, pessimistic, consists of "condemning part of the global labor force to precariousness, while subjecting the other part to a leisure activity that produces value," to use the author's critical formulation. The second, more optimistic, inspires us with this question: Working without knowing it, producing value without seeming to do so—while being distracted by "gamified" interfaces, or surreptitiously agglomerating knowledge collectives likely in the long run to constitute knowledge that can be shared ad infinitum—is this not a glimpse of possible new forms of work organization, more contributive and empowering, finally overcoming commonplace relations of subordination?

The Malevolence of Robots

Alexei Grinbaum, *Les Robots et le Mal*[18] (Desclée de Brouwer, 2018).

In the economic press, we generally associate technology (i.e., the technology found in hospitals) in our means of transport and in our communication tools with the idea of good, or failing that, with the idea of progress. However, as Alexei Grinbaum, a researcher at the French Atomic Energy Commission, notes, this is not always the case:

> Domestic helpers become informers, autonomous cars suddenly kill, conversational agents insult their interlocutors. Computer systems participate in human conflicts, and sometimes provoke them.

In short, technology can cause good as well as evil, "break an arm, cause an accident, insult us or give us bad advice."

This essay attempts to continue the work carried out by the Institute for the Future of Mankind at Oxford University, devoted to the "malicious use of artificial intelligence." A recent report from the institute, available online,[19] highlights the vulnerabilities of computer systems and the need to preventively rethink our digital, physical, and political security. The author also points out that the word "malicious" is a kind of a confession from the report's authors: like Descartes's "evil genius," the use of this word says a lot about the risks of violence contained in the use of our so-called intelligent machines, smartphones, or personal assistants. Grinbaum explores three theses in a bid to shed light on our relationship with these tools.

The first is a reminder that the notions of good and evil are in themselves foreign to robots of any kind. If machines do "evil," they do so perfectly innocently, we might say, or rather in perfect ignorance. Machines only produce abstract data and codes that improve the performance of certain industrial processes, without having the ability to grasp their ultimate goal.

The second is that machines do not deserve to be accused of anything, because they are not a subject of law. Law and ethics characterize us as human beings, and machines should not, and cannot, substitute for us in making moral choices.

The third thesis stems from the first two: only recourse to chance—that is to say, beyond good and evil—could emancipate the machine from the choices that are ultimately ours. This recourse to randomness is the only way to give back unto Caesar what belongs to him—that is to say, to give back to humans the ethical choices that only they are in a position to make.

The solution Grinbaum proposed may appear shocking, in that it privileges chance over transparency, whereas the latter is nowadays increasingly demanded by users themselves. He takes the example of Microsoft, which had committed itself to pure, perfect transparency in the traceability of data linked to artificial intelligence, before changing its mind and noting, as the CNIL[20] itself finally admits, that "this is an unattainable desire par excellence." To explain this, the author argues that deep learning processes, the permanent learning of machines, cannot be clearly represented by human intelligence.

This reflection prompts us to question the growing space, already noted by Günther Anders in the 1950s, that exists between the multiple possibilities of machine intelligence and the limits of our reasoning capacities. This should encourage us to put at the top of our agendas the definition of ideas that we wish to defend through using these tools. From this angle, Grinbaum offers a maxim that should be meditated upon by organizations that want to take advantage of the possibilities offered by AI but also by the engineering and management schools that train their future project managers: "Every project is thought through before it is carried out: it is during this time of reflection that ethics takes over."

NOTES

1. *Siliconization of the world.*
2. https://mastersofscale.com.
3. *Dictionary of Common Goods.*
4. See G. Hardin, *The Tragedy of the Commons*, trans. Laurent Bury, ed. and commentary Dominique Bourg (Paris: PUF, 2018).
5. *House of Social and Innovative Economies.*
6. *Homo detritus. Criticism of the waste society.*
7. Institut Francilien Recherche Innovation Société, https://ifris.org.
8. It was better before.
9. A reference to the General Charles de Gaulle.
10. "You have to adapt." On a new political imperative.
11. What do algorithms dream of? Our lives in the age of big data.
12. The war of intelligences.
13. Algorithmic Life. Critique of numerical reasoning.
14. https://criticalengineering.org/fr.
15. *The Civilisation of the Goldfish.* A short treatise on the attention market.
16. One of the largest free-to-air TV networks in Europe in terms of audience figures.
17. *Waiting for the robots.* A clic work survey.
18. *Robots and evil.*
19. https://www.fhi.ox.ac.uk/new-report-malicious-use-ai/
20. National Commission for Information Technology and Freedom, https://www.cnil.fr/en/home.

Chapter 3

Loss of Meaning or a Need for More Humanities?

This section opens with a discussion of an essay that struck a chord with many readers recently: *La Révolte des premiers de la classe* (Rebellion of the Nerds). The book looks at young university graduates opting for surprising professional careers, generally in a field far removed from their initial training. These chain reactions to what David Graeber calls bullshit jobs allow us to question the meaning of working life in a context in which burnout and brownout have become endemic, as numerous scientific and philosophical studies have shown.[1]

ON THE "SEARCH FOR MEANING" AT WORK

We need to take this movement seriously, and that will require more than simply appointing a "chief happiness officer"—a recent fad intended to assuage the suffering of managers, whose limitations are laid bare by Edgar Cabanas and Eva Illouz. Another timely critique comes courtesy of Benoît Heilbrunn, a philosopher of market phenomena, in his analysis of how brands substitute the signifier for the signified, and when, in a more psychoanalytical register, the coauthors of *Psychoanalyzing organizations* evoke the production of affects linked to professional life.

Of course, the question of happiness cannot be neglected in organizations, if it can be neglected at all, given our deepest human motivations. But perhaps it is time for an even more critical reassessment of the traditional wage labor model. This is what Bernard Stiegler proposes in his short essay on the need for us to unlearn and reinvent our relationship with machines, particularly with automation. Such a method seems to me preferable to the more eagerly awaited speeches on "humanistic enterprises" and "fulfillment through the search for meaning" as proposed by Jacques Lecomte and Aaron Hurst respectively, who seem to believe, a little too quickly, that we all have an easy, authentic relationship with ourselves.

This is not an opinion shared by the dozen or so social scientists engaged in a comprehensive analysis of what they call "emotional commodities." Their analyses show that we are apparently no longer capable of knowing what we really feel, so much so that our emotions are guided by a marketing of excitement that produces emotions for us. Moreover, as Yves Citton's analysis shows, the whole media system is concerned here, in its propensity to radically influence the ways we act and think (or not).

So, how can we regain privileged access to our "inner voice"? The work of the psychologist and anthropologist Victor Rosenthal shows that this is perhaps our best hope for effective decision making and choosing the right direction. This double voice, absent from management and leadership manuals, is still what distinguishes us from the machines around us. But that is not all: as the philosopher Robert Misrahi highlights, happiness (at work), or rather joy, according to his own terminology, is also conquered by the triumph of freedom. Unless empathy, as discussed by Paul Bloom, or talent, an inescapable notion in the current discourse of "human resources" managers, to which sociologist Pierre-Michel Menger devotes a study, somehow become the gold standard against which the industrial and human success of organizations are measured.

But to rediscover the meaning of work, we should perhaps begin by rediscovering the "meaning of thought," as Gabriel Markus indicates, or perhaps even the lost sense of interiority, scattered by the digital age, which lends its title to *The Future of Interiority in the Age of New Technologies*. The authors of the latter tome insist heavily on the words "modesty" and "tact," in short, savoir-vivre, a lost art that managers would be wrong to neglect entirely.

Against Bullshit Jobs, the Revenge of Jobs Hic and Nunc

Jean-Laurent Cassely, *La Révolte des premiers de la classe. Métiers à la con, quête de sens et reconversions urbaines*[2] (Arkhé, 2017).

In 1988, the philosopher and journalist André Gorz anticipated the description of what David Graeber calls "bullshit jobs":

> Work has disappeared because life has withdrawn from the universe. There are no more people; only numbers chasing numbers in silence, unquestionable because they are insensitive, mute. At the end of his day, the operator gets up. Nothing remains of what he has done, no visible, measurable material assets: he has achieved nothing. But this nothing has exhausted him.[3]

Thirty years later, it is unfortunate but undeniable that many professions, not least of all management, are increasingly subject to stress, fatigue, and burnout. It is hard not to wonder whether certain traditional forms of management need a rethink and whether it might not finally be time to move on from Taylor, as I proposed in *Postcritical Management Studies: Philosophical Investigations*,[4] by putting individuals and their aspirations back at the center of managerial processes.

Jean-Laurent Cassely's work opens a gap, surprising in more way than one, in these models of the past. What is it all about? It is about a growing minority of young university graduates taking control of their professional lives and refusing to submit to the rigors of the bureaucratic world, choosing instead to become neo-merchants or neo-artisans, or both: pastry chefs, itinerant restaurant owners, cheese makers, butchers, florists, wine merchants, coffee roasters. It would be wrong to consider this insubordination as anecdotal. We are talking very seriously about a hipster economy that brings together a willingness to undertake ways of developing its activity on new bases, quality rather than quantity, singularism and a taste for rarity rather than unbridled commercialism, local anchoring rather than massive expansion.

These academically gifted refuseniks are leading the way in more than one respect: they use technology to their advantage; with crowdfunding, for example, they create new "values," especially urban ones, by putting them at the center of their activity; they are reinventing craft trades that had fallen out of favor, making them upmarket concerns. In short, they use their managerial skills for more subjective and often more subtle purposes. They are also adapting to the rise of artificial intelligence, which they know eventually will trivialize some of their technical skills in the service sector. Their antidote: creating hic et nunc rather than feeling sorry for themselves by anticipation.

We can, of course, make fun of this post-hipster phenomenon, with its wide-eyed enthusiasm for the food trade or the revival of cabinetmaking. "Oh, what a beautiful chicken leg! Oh, what a beautiful lampshade!" But, as the saying goes, "when the wise man points at the moon, the fool looks at the finger." What appeals to these bright, young things is not so much the return to the product as the lived experience of reconnecting with oneself and others in a more direct, often more human model of customer relations, as witnessed by actress Jennifer Dundas, creator of Blue Marble ice creams. Escaping the rigid systems of evaluation that were hindering their motivation, these good students approach their work with renewed zeal. And affectio societatis.

These freelance business enthusiasts, who represent fewer than 20 percent of higher education graduates, and the empowering experiences to which they testify eventually may be followed by many others. It may well begin to look like a case of revenge, but without resentment, allowing us to reformulate André Gorz's observations for a new era:

> Life has reappeared in the place of production, and our expectations of autonomy and reflexivity are not disappointed. Our projects succeed without the Excel spreadsheet taking too large a part in them. Abstract work has basically been transformed into real work and, as if by some miracle, the procedural professionals have disappeared. At the end of the day, in spite of the difficulties, there is a whiff of revenge in the air; the revenge of a generation that, step by step, is reinventing our relationship with work.

Happycratia: The (Desperate) Management of One's Happiness

Edgar Cabanas and Eva Illouz, *Manufacturing Happy Citizens: How the Science and Industry of Happiness Control Our Lives* (Polity, 2019).

Is the presence of a chief happiness officer, who is supposed to create the necessary conditions for happiness in French companies and some Belgian administrations, really surprising? The idea that employee motivation is the main factor in the success of an organization is not new; the idea that their well-being is the source of it, as well as their loyalty or commitment, is not really surprising either. Where yesterday's HR managers promised breaks and organized fitness trips for their teams, today's CHOs plan happy hours and set up indoor sport subscriptions. Plus ça change, plus c'est la même chose.

It is precisely this permanence that comes as a surprise. Why take up, and now in an "official" way, a question as universal as that of happiness? Could it be a tacit admission that companies have so far failed in their promise of happiness, as the phenomena of bore-out or brown-out indicate?

Edgar Cabanas and Eva Illouz point out that today, under the influence of positive psychology, we are witnessing the development of the happiness industry in all directions: applications for smartphones such as Happify, publications on the subject—more than two hundred on Amazon have the word in their titles—seminars promising personal development and help for oneself, access to online communities such as Possibility of change . . . all of this is growing and thriving.

With these new tools, the goal is to upend Maslow's sacrosanct pyramid of needs: in this new context it is not success that leads to personal fulfillment but vice versa. Because you are the personified ideal of sustainable well-being, you will soon be successful. The formula for happiness ultimately goes something like this: start by being happy, and everything will be fine.

Barbara Fredrickson, one of the key authors in this fast-developing field of research, even extends this reasoning to the private sphere when she explains that "successful marriages are characterised by a positivity/

negativity ratio of about 5:1, while marriages that go from bad to worse, up to final separation, show a ratio of about 1:1." Today, positive psychology even has its own publications, such as the *Journal of Happiness Studies*. According to the authors, more than sixty thousand different studies have been carried out in this field in the space of a few years . . . alas, without any conclusive results.

This lack of scientific heft can be ascribed to at least three factors: the first is its naive obviousness. Admittedly, "the weekend is more fun than Thursday, bad weather affects morale, Christmas Day is one of the happiest days of the year, depressed people prefer darker shades," and so on and so forth . . . but none of this tells us anything.

Second, Cabanas and Illouz note an aporia of reasoning: one should constantly take care of oneself and try to transform oneself, even though the aim of the whole affair is paradoxically to reach a sort of nirvana where the personality has attained full completion by disappearing.

Last, but not least, one final point is problematic: we forget that in our most everyday feelings, we have a positive and a negative side: happy to leave a job, for example, but sad to leave behind esteemed colleagues. If happiness is the gateway to all happiness, then what can we say to those who are unhappy? And what should we say to ourselves when we are unhappy in our turn? To think otherwise would be to disregard the ambivalence and complexity of human feelings.

These three points stand, but the authors would do well to remember that the question of happiness is less trivial than they seem to think. Could it be replaced by "justice, prudence, solidarity or even loyalty," they ask? It would be without mentioning the fact that no factor in human history has ever been more essential and structuring than the search for happiness. As Blaise Pascal timelessly put it,

> All men want to be happy. This is without exception. . . . It is the motive for all the actions of all men. Even those who are going to hang themselves.

It is understood that suicide appears to the person who has recourse to it as a lesser suffering than that of continuing the course of his or her life.

Will happiness remain a goal for all of us, outside the boundaries of organizations as well as within them? It seems a safe bet that research of this type in economics, management sciences, sociology, and elsewhere will continue to proliferate, without at any time taking the trouble to define the notion. Unless perhaps we should be satisfied with the aphorism that Don Draper proffered in *Mad Men*:

Happiness is that moment before you need even more happiness.

The End of the Old World of Brands and Marketing

Benoît Heilbrunn, *Méditations marchandes*[5] (Le Bord de l'eau, 2018).

Why do we put desire into buying a specific brand of toothpaste, shampoo, or soap, and other products that we know are fundamentally uninteresting? Why on earth do we think that a cleaning product for our kitchens and bathrooms will be more effective if it is scented with calendula or lime? Why are smokers unable to recognize their favorite brand in a blind taste test? It is, explains Benoît Heilbrunn, because the "trademark society has substituted the sign for the meaning" or, he writes, because the product has become "a way of dressing objects." So much so that we have long since entered a society where the practical value of goods is secondary to their symbolic value.

The author of this work, singular in many ways, presents himself both as a professor of marketing and as a philosopher of market phenomena. The aim here is not to popularize already-dominant trends in American marketing thinking, based on a few clichés gleaned here and there, but on the contrary to provide a new, ironic, and affable, critical and clinical look at brand strategy and its repercussions on our consumption behavior.

To do this, Heilbrunn turns to continental philosophy: Derrida, Lévi-Strauss, Baudrillard, Stiegler, and even Bataille, who perceived better than anyone, and before the prodigious development of the luxury industry, that "unproductive expenditure has its own ends."[6] Kant himself, according to the author, remarked that "the main trick" of these messages is to persuade "each consumer that he is an aesthete and an expert, while bombarding him with products with standardised tastes." In short, some of Europe's sharpest minds are used here to decipher the decisive decoding of this society "of well-being, of living well together," and of the "sharing of values" that today's advertising messages, which can be consulted ad infinitum on our screens, seek to embody.

Benoît Heilbrunn highlights the extent to which consumer issues are, indeed, social issues when he invites us to meditate on the results of a study according to which, "on certain Wednesdays, children aged between 6 and 12 can swallow up to one hundred and ninety-two commercials during a day of watching television," or when he notes that an individual is "on average exposed each day to almost two thousand logos." This "MacDonaldization" of the world, as Ritzer puts it, is a method of remotely controlling the lives of we the consumers, and the author does a convincing job of demonstrating its limitations impending transformation.

In fact, this change is already at work. Using a few examples, Heilbrunn shows us that brands are reinventing themselves differently, starting from scratch. He cites the example of Hermé, turning cakes into an artform with boutiques that look like galleries, or of Hermès, whose communication has turned its back entirely on the past, which he calls overdifferentiation and over-semantization. To this he strangely contrasts the "dullness of the brand," which reminds us "of a game of transparency between air and water," a reference "to the fecund categories of Chinese pictorial art: the vague, the indistinct or the contemplative."

For Heilbrunn, the twenty-first century will be the age of the Chinese brand: it will no longer be a question of superimposing its values through a combative, repetitive discourse but of making the essence of the brand discreetly recognized. Expect to see Sun Tzu's *The Art of War* quietly replace Kotler[7] on the bedside table of future marketing students.

Ultimately, through a series of subtle touches, this book helps us decipher how brands determine our ways of seeing and thinking. Above all, it invites us to mobilize our thinking to help us apprehend marketing with concepts in line with the imperatives of the future.

Psychoanalyzing Organizations

Gilles Arnaud, Pascal Fugier, and Bénédicte Vidaillet, *Psychanalyse des organizations. Théorie, clinique, interventions*[8] (Érès, 2018).

We know that for Sigmund Freud, three professions were impossible: government, education, and psychoanalysis. We should, therefore, be skeptical, to say the least, of a book that seeks to persuade us of the contributions of psychoanalysis, considered as a medical science, to the study of organizations and their modes of governance. It is, however, this difficult task that the three coauthors of this book have set for themselves.

In fact, the founder of the discipline added the qualifier "almost" to this witticism, and it is into the interval of this quasi-impossibility that the editors of this important psychoanalytical tome plunge, for our benefit. This book is important for at least two reasons. First, for its synthetic overview of many currents of post-Freudian thought: psychoanalysis applied to small groups, for example, via the Lacanian approach, clinical sociology, or socio-psychoanalysis. This concern for completeness reinforces the overall strength of the book and complements its second great asset: the authors offer a reading of organizational behavior that is totally different from mainstream interpretations, which are most often quantitativist or cognitivist and too often beset by delusions of scientific accuracy. The book thus reveals, in its multiple expressions and its own complexity, the place of the irrational and the unconscious in the functioning of organizations.

The book is thus presented as an extension of the main Freudian intuitions, even extending into the field of social groups, notably expressed in *Totem and Taboo*. It is a question of taking up again the great classical notions (the transfer, the desire, or the symptom) in a perspective that leaves room for something other than individual analysis because it extends to the psychology of "organized crowds." The idea that the constitution of groups creates in itself a new regime of emotions establishes a relational vision of individuals. The principle of demonstration is based on the following bias: in "finalized social entities," individuals are never psychologically separated from each other.

This resonates well with the approaches to leadership proposed by Kets de Vries and Miller, who describe organizations using five neurotic styles: paranoid, compulsive, theatrical, depressive, and schizoid, trying to show the positive and negative side of each. For the paranoid style, for example, the organization certainly shows itself capable of anticipating potential risks, but the paranoid organization is also where a climate of mistrust prevails. Yannis Gabriel, for his part, develops a theory of leadership that projects two types of fantasies: that of the leader as a "primal fusional mother" and that of the leader as a "primal omnipotent father." As for Vincent de Gaulejac, he brings together the findings of clinical sociology to highlight the fundamental copartnership of the social and the psychic.

These psychoanalytical schools could ultimately be criticized for remaining a little too far removed from philosophical criticism, that of Jaspers, Ricoeur, or Wittgenstein, for example. But that would be without counting the chapter devoted to the psychodynamics of work, as proposed by Christophe Dejours, which offers a decisive direction: by drawing more extensively than his predecessors on the concepts of phenomenology (with specific reference to Maurice Merleau-Ponty and Michel Henry), Dejours produces a theory that leaves a central place to the body and the production of affects linked to professional activity. This approach appears necessary, as the ontological and psycho-physiological levels of suffering, a major phenomenon of contemporary managerial reality, are so intimately linked.

Finally, this current of research, while agreeing with Freud, at the same time proves him at least a little bit wrong: the psychoanalysis of organizations, a study that seemed almost impossible to the Viennese master to carry out, becomes a practicable activity. And even a shareable one.

"Humanist Companies": Combining Profession and Passion

Jacques Lecomte, *Les Entreprises humanistes : comment elles vont changer le monde*[9] (Les Arènes, 2016).

One can conceive of one's professional activity in three ways: as a job to pay the bills; as a career, where everyone is aiming for a new promotion; or as a vocation. In the latter case, it is self-actualization that becomes the major axis of professional activity. When a vocation becomes just a job, we are faced with an antihumanist managerial perspective. On the other hand, when a job becomes a vocation, then the humanist aim of the organization is fully revealed.

For Jacques Lecomte, who devotes a volume to what he calls "humanist companies," this mutation is possible and is based on three modes of thought that can be considered as management principles: positive psychology, which focuses on what makes human beings happier and more optimistic; convivial-ity; and human kindness, which he mentions in his previous work. Convivi-alism is this current of thought associated with the sociologist Alain Caillé, founded upon the four principles of common humanity, common sociality, individualization, and controlled opposition.

The main thrust of this reflection centered on humanism in organizations revolves concretely around a critique of homo œconomicus, who still believes that others are motivated only by money, while what we really need to do is think more seriously about fulfillment at work. The idea is to implement a method of team management based on "appreciative inquiry," in which giv-ing value to the actions of others is always important, whatever they may be. The whole approach is based on a heliotropic principle that, as the author explains, establishes an analogy between plants and humans:

Just as a plant turns toward the sun, individuals mobilize if they have the prospect of a positive vision and if they rely on the luminous part of themselves.

These proposals, however positive they may be, are nevertheless question-able on at least two grounds. The first concerns this Rousseauism, which sees in humanity only a kind of goodness . . . when we know that organizations, and herein lies the whole problem, are also the scene of power struggles, battles of egos and divergent interests. The "resentful" are never completely absent from organizational life, to paraphrase Arthur Schopenhauer, a pessi-mistic philosopher if ever there was one, who nonetheless receives a citation in this book.

The second reason is that Lecomte considers happiness an a priori method rather than a result. Success and satisfaction are sometimes achieved by working on the negative, on contradiction, through negative emotions such as uncertainty or exasperation. Perhaps this is the reason why, as Lecomte modestly claims, "there are few scientific studies evaluating the effects of the appreciative process. Moreover," he admits, "this may be an inherent limita-tion of the method itself."

On the other hand, we can agree with the author on a very Stendhalian idea taken up by Roland Barthes: the most beautiful gift one can give to a person is, indeed, the combination of a profession and a passion.

The Purpose Economy: Flourishing through the Search for Meaning

Aaron Hurst, *The Purpose Economy: How Your Desire for Impact, Personal Growth and Community Is Changing the World* (Boise: Elevate, 2014).

What if the meaning of working life, the meaning we give to the efforts we make at work, were to become the heart of economic development? This question, which may seem a little utopian to a European, is posed by an American essayist in the second edition of his book, *Purpose Economy*. For Aaron Hurst, indeed, the information economy, that of dashboards and performance indicators, is undergoing radical change. This revolution is that of going beyond the rationality of means, methods, and techniques, notably embodied by the figure of the manager, to the logic of ethical and ecological ends.

In short, our need to enrich our relationships with others and to participate in the development of humanity may be taking precedence over all other considerations. The author recalls the results of two oft-cited studies: one published by academics from Princeton University, which showed that beyond $75,000 in annual income, people's moods and satisfaction no longer change; and a study compiled by PricewaterhouseCoopers for the latest World Economic Forum, which showed that consumers are themselves in search of meaning, which they value over price and functionality.

The reasoning consists in showing that the global development of nonprofit activities, in which Hurst is a specialist, is having consequences beyond the nonprofit domain. The essayist cites many companies whose success depends on this community or ecological concern, such as Seventh Generation, a manufacturer of biodegradable hygiene products for children; the Khan Academy, which has delivered three hundred thousand free lessons since its inception and reaches ten million students worldwide; the KickStarter platform, which supports and finances artistic and cultural projects; or Medium, which allows young authors to receive comments from their peers directly online.

This enthusiasm needs tempering, for at least two reasons: the first is the vagueness of this notion of purpose, which can be said to concern all companies that have a certain drive, an intent, a direction, or an idea intended to benefit the community. But in this case, what are the criteria for validly distinguishing a good purpose from a bad one? The author is imprecise on this important point, even though it is supposed to determine the entire method.

The second aspect concerns the ambition of this book, which is also to fight against the feeling of 70 percent of people who, according to a Gallup study, say they feel detached from their work. Like many of his American contemporaries, Hurst is optimistic that research in positive psychology can help in this respect. Of course, making organizational life more humanly satisfying is a significant goal for management studies; but to distinguish at this point between organizations, considering some as a place of distress and others as a place of intense pleasure, cannot be a plausible starting point. It is also important to know how to live with negative emotions, sadness, anger, or uncertainty, which are not only part of our humanity, but are often the ultimate resource that enables organizations to avoid making irreparable mistakes.

This book prophecies the imminent demise of management, a claim that is surely exaggerated. Surely it is the role of enlightened management to reconcile these two points: the aims of the organization and respect for the diversity of its members.

"Emotional Goods" and Emotional Marketing

Eva Illouz, ed., *Emotions as Commodities* (Routledge, 2019).

What happens when we feel an emotion directly related to an act of consumption? In this case, are our emotions still our own? Consider a few concrete examples: if we watch a horror film, it's to play at being afraid. If we choose to go to Club Med for our next holidays, it's to enjoy some time devoid of the slightest feeling of guilt, whatever we do. If we listen to a playlist compiled for newly divorced people (yes, there is such a thing), it's to try to drum up positive vibes again.

It is, however, generally accepted that ultimately only our emotions are our own, and that only our genuinely experienced emotions allow us to recognize ourselves. If I laugh or cry, if I am sad or happy, I assume by definition that I am the one who feels the need for these states. My truth is what I feel deep inside myself. But, as all these examples show, we are, in fact, constantly coproducing affects, guided by commercial or medical offers, for instance, which intensify within ourselves feelings that are no longer entirely our own.

This phenomenon of "emotional capitalism" is described in a collective work by the sociologist Eva Illouz, who challenges the idea that the economic sphere deprives us of our feelings. She even supports the opposite proposition: never before have our emotional resources been such a subject of interest to advertisers. We can see this with the continuous development of relational, sensorial, or experiential marketing. To put it in the words of the philosopher Axel Honneth, who provides the preface for her: the more "social behaviours are recoverable and recuperated . . . , the more we are losing our ability to distinguish between feelings that are really experienced and feelings that are the result of manipulation." Consumption and acting on oneself become consubstantial, to the point that it is marketers, and perhaps also psychoanalysts, who, without knowing it, stimulate and define our experience of pleasure, disgust, or good conscience.

"Laughter is the best medicine," reads a get-well-soon card; there is no need to write it down anymore, because Hallmark does it for us. Friendship, or concern for others, has in a way become a commodity like any other, what Illouz and her coauthors call an emotional commodity: our emotions are thus objects like any other, which can be exchanged, quantified—that is to say, manipulated ad infinitum.

This book confirms what we have known in management since the 1930s and the development of the school of "human relations," which highlighted, notably in the Hawthorne experiments developed by Elton Mayo, that human behavior is largely determined by our psychology. We speak today of "emotional intelligence" (Daniel Goleman) to evoke the essential quality of a good manager—namely, the ability to manage, to evaluate one's own feelings, even if it means transforming them artificially, as well as those of the members of one's team. Emotions are in some ways more akin to a skill than a personal experience.

We might also extend this observation into the artistic domain: What defines a good filmmaker, or a good painter, if not the power to move us? The question now is whether each of us still has the means to escape the intoxication of our sensibility by industrial, artistic, or medical marketing, other than by denouncing immaterial capitalism, as this book does. In short, can we still save our authenticity within systems of influence that are gradually eroding it away?

Let's hope that it is still possible to protect ourselves against false emotions, by reading books like this one, for example, but also by ensuring the quality of our cultural consumption, the preservation of the secrecy of our personal data, or the ability to disconnect from smartphones to better reconnect with ourselves. Because authenticity requires us to rediscover our relationship with our emotions, to truly experience and feel them, as well as our reasoning capacities.

"Mediarchy": Information or Manipulation?

Yves Citton, *Médiarchie* (Seuil, "La couleur des idées," 2017).

"The media don't inform us, they make us aware." So, in somewhat simplified form, goes the thesis presented in this book by Yves Citton, professor at Paris 8 University and specialist in information and communication sciences. With the term "mediarchy," the author designates "the primary power, originating from the medium understood as a means of communication, over those who believe they use it within a milieu of perception that in reality this medium conditions." In other words, the tools that media organizations believe they use to inform and entertain us in fact determine the forms of attention we reserve for them, and in fine delimit, without our discernment, what it is important to know or not to know in the news. In this way, Citton shows us why we have less control than ever over our beliefs and aspirations. He notes, for example, that, "since Google and Facebook algorithms govern so much of our perceptions of the world, it is incomparably more problematic not to have access to how they work than not being able to lift the bonnet of a car."

Theodor Adorno, Guy Debord, Noam Chomsky, and Bernard Stiegler have all denounced the power relations that are part of our media practices and prevent us from accessing reality, both political and socioeconomic. Here, the originality of the approach is to give pride of place to a sort of synthesis of non-French-speaking scientific works and publications (German, Italian, or English) treating the media as a "milieu" in which we evolve, think, and act. We discover a renewed look at the media in general, whose main characteristic is, Citton warns us, to "produce audiences" from the "coalescence of a community around shared vibrations, affections and concerns."

In the final section, the author makes several proposals, the most radical of which is certainly that of giving big data the status of "commons," considering them no longer as the property of a few multinationals but as an inalienable resource, like languages or oceans. The possible nationalization of Facebook or Google, or their transformation into public services, which is sometimes envisaged, would go in this direction.

However, the most striking proposal, following on Bernard Stiegler's work, is undoubtedly the need to envisage a pharmacological relationship to information: for the ancient Greeks, a pharmakon was a substance that both cures—a remedy—and harms—a poison. In short, we must be wary of "true information": that which leads us to believe that the forced handshake of two political leaders is more valuable than the Anthropocene evolution of the pH of the oceans or the quantity of nitrogen and sulphur circulating in certain large cities of the globe. It is, therefore, necessary to develop new ways of consuming and deciphering the automatisms and injunctions of media speech. For this, we are invited to consider the media, certainly as prostheses that prolong our mental capacities, as remedies for our physical and psychological deficiencies, but also as poisons that can make us fascinated and dependent.

At a time of fake news and post-interpretation, it is worth returning to the words of the great Marshall McLuhan, the originator of the "global village" concept:

> Once we have surrendered our senses and nervous systems to private manipulation of those who would try to benefit from taking a lease on our eyes, and ears and nerves, we don't really have any rights left.[10]

"Collaborate" with Your Inner Voice

Victor Rosenthal, *Quelqu'un à qui parler. Une histoire de la voix intérieure*[11] (PUF, 2019).

It is an experience we have all encountered upon entering a subway car or walking in the street: people talking to themselves, with nobody else to hear. We know that they are talking to their headphones, and we can assume, or at least hope, that they are not completely alone, nor completely crazy. But, come to think of it, is talking to oneself really a sign of madness?

This is not the opinion of Victor Rosenthal, psychologist and anthropologist in charge of research at the Inserm,[12] in this beautiful study devoted to the speech we address to ourselves. Through in-depth analysis, he demonstrates that discussion with oneself is a necessary condition for our ability to think about the world we live in. The fictitious companion inside my head, this second voice I hear when I speak to myself, is precisely what makes it possible to communicate with oneself, but also with the outside world. Whether it's a soliloquy, for example, the story of how I feel at the end of a bad day's work, or a clamor such as "Watch out!" that I address myself to avoid being hit by a car, each time this vocal phenomenon occurs it offers a reminder of the sort of cohabitation that exists between the person I am and the person who never stops addressing me.

Conversing with this second voice has been going on since well before the time of subway cars, or indeed streets. The ancient Greeks, especially the Stoics, had already recognized it in the form of the daemon, that almost divine force that shows us the path to follow, the program of daily action, the roadmap that belongs only to oneself. Moreover, philosophical practice itself was then subject to the condition of a relationship with oneself, a dialogue with oneself, a relationship of the soul with itself. Listening to oneself meant listening to a voice other than our own, which speaks to us and we alone can hear, in both senses of the word. This voice can be subvocalized or vocalized, incarnated and audible, as Rosenthal reminds us, using the example of a mother who pretends to speak to her children when her words are intended only for herself . . . because only she can understand them.

This self-narrative, which our inner voice constantly reveals and shapes, is important for all those in influential social positions, for at least three reasons.

The first is that, without this voice that affirms or confirms, there is no decision: "Only one voice, an intimate voice, can validly make resolutions," the author reminds us. Deciding essentially means agreeing with oneself, evaluating situations from different points of view, something that the sheer haste of our will cannot hope to achieve with wisdom or reason. This split voice, which we encounter, for example, in writing a diary that reveals in written form what we are unable to say to ourselves, is also the voice that calls out to us, that warns us or reassures us about the commitments we make.

Basically, this voice acts as a decision-making tool because it is also the voice of others that speaks within us. This inner voice bears the hallmarks of social life: it provides a level of dialogue that allows each person to be understood by others, to be audible to the other members of the group to which one belongs. Convincing in business or politics requires first listening to this voice, which forces us to take an interest in something other than ourselves.

The second reason is related to the first, in that it is also the condition for all ethical behavior. As Socrates noted, this other voice within me reminds me of my commitments: this imperative voice is the one that has the strength to remind us, when necessary, of the fulfillment of our duties.

Finally, "the inner voice has the power to put imagination at the service of action. . . . And the characteristic of this vocal imagination is that it is not like a daydream." In fact, in the management of organizations, no quality is more precious than the exercise of the imagination, which only an effort of duplication, contradiction, and sometimes internal conflict can produce.

It is precisely this awakening of the heart and intelligence that accompanies this voice that sets us apart from machines. Artificial intelligence, despite its undeniable power, does not have this virtue. No one to talk to, to rectify a trajectory or branch off before it is too late. While in every one of us, the daemon continues unceasingly to instruct our skills and consciences. It is what allows us to coexist advantageously with the world, with others, and with ourselves.

Managers between Constraint, Imitation and Imagination

Robert Misrahi, *La Liberté. Le pouvoir de créer*[13] (Autrement, 2018).

In classic management studies, the manager, the so-called decision maker, is often defined as an autonomous subject, capable of making strategic and other forks; he is a "guiding hand," capable of steering or redirecting the course of things within an organization.

In contemporary philosophy, these assertions provoke a wry smile. For some of the dominant currents of continental philosophy, in the work of Lacan or Deleuze, for example, the autonomous subject is a farce: there are only impulses, forces in presence, relations between beings and things. The free and autonomous subject, in management as elsewhere, is under the permanent fire of philosophical and psychoanalytical criticism.

If the general orientation of these philosophies is right, then we need to thoroughly review the definitions of management, as well as its traditions. Let us propose here a redefinition centered around three terms that are supposed to say everything about managerial power: constraint, imitation, and imagination. The latter is central here; it can be understood as the faculty of change and innovation, allowing us to loosen the grip of the first two terms. But then, if freedom is inaccessible to managers, are we not condemned to the exercise of constraint and mimicry as the only possible horizons for the act of managing?

In this short essay, Robert Misrahi, a philosopher specializing in Sartre and Spinoza, attempts to liberate us from philosophical determinism in all its forms and to reconnect with freedom. He thus sacrifices "residual Marxism," "conquering psychoanalysis," "field sociology," and, generally speaking, all those disciplines that display the "presumption of being sciences" but "are all silent on the question of the subject and its vocation to true freedom and joy."

For Misrahi, in fact, it is necessary to reconstruct a philosophy of the subject, of the one who enjoys, who suffers, who speaks, and who acts, to better combat the "monumental retrospective illusion" of which deterministic philosophies are victims. They would certainly like to change the world so that it is better while, at the same time, announcing in advance that this is impossible. It is in this respect that this specialist of Spinoza is heterodox to say the least, insofar as, for him, the belief in determinism "is nothing but ignorance of the causes (and reasons) that make us act." It should be remembered that, for Spinoza indeed, it was on the contrary "ignorance of the causes which determine us," and "let us believe that we are free."

This is why we should not blame the economic sciences or the economists for being wrong all the time in their forecasts. Their mistakes do not in any way condemn their presuppositions, because everything ultimately depends on what the players in economic life decide to do with their power of imagination—everything that, by definition, economics can never decide for them. For these actors, managers as well as executives, imagination, the author claims, remains a "consubstantial power of consciousness," which "anticipates (time), sees (form and colours), loves (desires and 'invests'), and reasons." It is therefore necessary, Misrahi affirms, to prioritize the effectiveness and fruitfulness of acts of creation, because they are what make us free and joyful.

Against Empathy, This "Vast Hypocrisy"?

Paul Bloom, *Against Empathy, The Case for Rational Compassion* (New York: HarperCollins, 2016).

"We're not dying of AIDS as much as we are from 11 years of Government neglect." Bill Clinton responded to this memorable remark by a member of Act-Up in 1992 with a phrase at least as famous: "I feel your pain." The future president thus meant a commonplace idea: the world would be a better place if everyone empathized, starting with the political staff and the economic decision makers. A few months later, Clinton became the forty-second president of the United States of America, winning the election comfortably.

Paul Bloom, a specialist in cognitive science at Yale University, takes the counterpoint to this posture, boldly declaring himself to be against empathy. According to him, being possessed by the feelings of others has several drawbacks and problems.

First, feeling what others feel is no guarantee of kindness. Bloom takes the example of psychopaths, who are distinguished precisely by the fact that they use the feelings of their victims to increase the cruelty of their actions.

Second, empathy leads us to worry about the immediate without being usefully aware of causes that may seem more distant but may have much more important consequences. We overestimate the here and now, to the detriment of long-term causes and consequences, such as global warming or the national debt rate. These are all things that deserve our vigilance but nevertheless leave us more or less indifferent because, compared to the shared feelings of everyday life, they are, after all, only a "pale statistical abstraction." "Basically," explains Bloom, "empathy is of no help to us when it comes to major social issues."

Finally, the psychologist points out that it is not empathy that prompts us to act in favor of others but, rather, as some scientific experiments appear to show, out of duty and according to a principle of justice. However, for our author, this is still to be welcomed because our empathic capacities are generally limited to those we know, whereas a principle of justice can be applied beyond our immediate emotional circles.

In short, to be "effective altruists," to use again the expression of the Australian philosopher Peter Singer, Bloom advises us to rely on our intelligence rather than our affective capabilities. Reason thus has its own logic that the heart does not know.

But while we are on the subject of intelligence in matters of humanity, let us agree that two arguments put forward by the author limit his overall analysis: on the one hand, he rightly states that teachers of morals, as a series of studies have shown, do not behave better than anyone else in everyday life: "They don't call their mothers more, they don't give more money to good works, they don't return books to the library more on time than their colleagues." In short, their intelligence on the matter is of no help to them.

On the other hand, this psychologist notes that "he himself is more disturbed when his internet connection becomes slow than when he hears on television that a tragedy has taken place in a country he has never heard of before." It is precisely because of a lack of empathy that a problem arises, because empathy should not be reserved for those close to us. Wouldn't its first register be rather to recognize in those a common humanity, what we sometimes dare in a republican regime to call our "brotherhood"?

Let's agree with Bloom on one point: the risk of empathy is the risk of barely concealed good conscience and hypocrisy. Blaise Pascal reminds us of this, as only he can:

> To pity the unfortunate is not contrary to lust. On the contrary, we can quite well give such evidence of friendship, and acquire the reputation of kindly feeling, without giving anything.

Is Talent Indispensable?

Pierre-Michel Menger, ed., *Le Talent en débat*[14] (PUF, 2018).

"Wherever I found talent and courage, I rewarded it. My principle was: a career open to talent." This sentence reported by one of Napoleon's doctors on St. Helena says a lot about the emperor's managerial ideas. In the conflict of values that has always raged in discussions of the subject, should talent, merit, or needs be favored in the attribution of rewards? Bonaparte answers without hesitation that the first choice is, when it comes to the qualitative evaluation of a person, preferable to any other.

In this, he was merely echoing what was already stated in the 1789 Declaration of Human Rights when it stated that "all citizens, being equal, are equally eligible for all public offices, places and offices, according to their capacity, and without distinction other than that of their virtues and talents." A reference that runs through Christian writing as well, notably in chapter 25 of the Gospel according to Matthew, in the passage known as "the parable of the talents."

It is interesting to note that this theme, important for management sciences, is making a strong comeback. It is no longer a question of managing human resources but, rather, of strengthening talent. This old theme has been revived since the end of the 1990s by the McKinsey consultancy firm under the name War for talent, where talent was recognized as a key factor in the success of an organization and, as a corollary, the importance of knowing how to develop the loyalty of those who are equipped with it.

In this book, based on papers from a colloquium held at the Collège de France in 2017 and chaired by sociologist Pierre-Michel Menger, readers are invited to take up this unavoidable theme by bringing it up to date and giving it a critical edge. As the author points out, talent, which is said in the same way in some forty languages, "is part of a range of concepts (as well as potential, skills, aptitudes, abilities) with which it is considered interchangeable in many studies in economics, management, psychology and education sciences." Unfortunately, its meaning is not very clear: talent can never be easily predicted but, as Menger rightly points out, "retrodirected." In the end, the person considered talented is the one who, in hindsight, is found to have confiscated most of the rewards for herself.

Faced with this major challenge for the management of contemporary organizations, Menger takes a point of view situated halfway between the two most common theoretical postulates: for some, talent is something innate, without really knowing what this original advantage is made up of. For others, the attribution of talent simply perpetuates relationships of domination that existed prior to its evaluation. As Pierre Bourdieu points out in his Rules of Art, "the dominant ones find nothing wrong with an order that consecrates them."[15] But, according to Menger, this Marxist-inspired option does not take sufficient account of the fact that the competitive testing of talent (i.e., its intersubjective validation), is what allows it to reveal itself as such. The egalitarian distribution of talent would, hypothetically, be a perilous utopia: What would happen, and in what world would we indeed live, if the possibility of distinguishing talent were no longer admitted?

For HR managers and consultants who are concerned about "keeping the career open to talent," the analyses in this book will allow them to climb to the top of the belfry and achieve the necessary critical distance from this voguish term. They will then realize, perhaps, that bringing together the best, in the form of profile matching, is sometimes the worst strategy for innovation, and that the objective of fair treatment of candidates during recruitment interviews, which aim, in the words of Jean-Louis Fabiani, "to transform micro-differences into macro-distinctions," is more difficult to implement than it seems. They will finally learn that talent is not necessarily synonymous with success, and that lack of talent is not a concern for everyone. They may draw solace, for example, from Kim Kardashian's signature on Twitter, shared with her fifty-nine million subscribers: #NotBadForAGirlWithNoTalent.

Intimacy and the Perils of the Digital Age

Éric Fiat and Jean-Christophe Valmette, eds., *Le Devenir de l'intériorité à l'heure des nouvelles technologies*[16] (Le Bord de l'eau, 2018).

What is inner life? When asked about this question by TV host Bernard Pivot in his program *Apostrophes* thirty years ago, Umberto Eco's answer was as follows: "Inner life is where there is no telephone." Alas, today we have the right to ask ourselves the painful question: Is there still a single place that does not have a telephone? Is it still possible to find a place, an anchorage, where everyone can find themselves alone without the interference of the gaze and judgment of others, without being seen, known, or heard by anyone other than oneself?

Claudine Haroche, anthropologist and research director at the CNRS,[17] who contributed to this collective work, seems to doubt it. Intimate life is undermined by a whole series of intrusive circumstances, not least among them mobile phones. Everything is now immediate and instantaneous, so much so that the relationship of the self to itself has become almost impossible. Focusing for a few moments on solving a problem seems to be a feat. The result is a self that is always available but fragmented, frayed, divided.

As the authors of this book, with its multiple approaches, point out, without a possible moment of imperceptibility and invisibility, the whole edifice of interior space falls apart. As a result, the freedom of each person, the very possibility of having an intimate conviction, is undermined. According to Serge Tisseron's expression, extimacy needs intimacy beforehand, just as light succeeds darkness, public space succeeds private space. A society that no longer needs padlocks would be like Bentham's famous panopticon: an infinite prison.

Paradoxically, however, in addition to this need for isolation, we feel the opposite, equally vital need: the need to be seen. For Rousseau, or closer to us, for Gaston Bachelard, without otherness our very humanity is put in default. Our identity is nothing if it is not recognized as such by others, in an ostensible manner: the literary character of Robinson Crusoe, who tries to fill the void that surrounds him, gives us a perfect illustration of this. This desire for recognition is thus seen as being constitutive of who we are in the eyes of others and of ourselves.

The future of interiority thus hinges on the question of what we choose to reveal of ourselves and what we prefer to preserve intimately. For the philosopher Éric Fiat, joint editor of this volume, this situation is typical of our inherent chiaroscuro us. In the end, this is a very moral question: Do we want the decent or the indecent? It's sometimes difficult to say because, as Fiat says, modesty depends on the environment in which one finds oneself: "in bourgeois families, one had to behave, now one has to 'let go.'" So, the virtue of modesty is only accessible to those who show practical wisdom, fair measure, exact proportion, mesotês (medium-term, middle ground), as Aristotle said.

What can a manager learn from these analyses? I have often put forward the idea that management, which comes from manus ("the hand," in Latin), was originally a kind of skill, delicacy, a form of tact. This is precisely what we are talking about here with modesty, which is just a way of behaving tactfully toward others. Éric Fiat finds the right words to describe one of the important facets of corporate manners:

> What the other hasn't hidden from me, I hide by not looking at her. I avert my gaze from what I am embarrassed to see.

THE SOUL REARMED?

Luc de Brabandère advised us to philosophize rather than to code: this is precisely what I would like to risk in this last section with authors who, to varying degrees, have tried to mobilize the humanities to, if not code the world, at least try to decode it. My selection opens with a pamphlet that has made history in the United States and only recently has been fully translated into French: *The Closing of the American Mind*, wherein Allan Bloom militates for philosophy as a source of creation of new worldviews (as well as the work on this subject coordinated by Deonna and Tieffenbach, discussed below), the only way, according to him, to direct collective action with any authority (in the positive sense suggested by Hannah Arendt). We shall then remain on the other side of the Atlantic with the postmodern theologian John Caputo, who, in a world grappling with fake news, reminds us of our duties of deliberation and interpretation. To escape the calculation programs committed to "predicting" our actions, our tastes, and our choices, Caputo encourages us to cultivate the weakness and doubt of those for whom nothing is ever a foregone conclusion.

For this to happen, however, the business schools and the universities must retain a place for the teaching of the humanities. Yet, the authors of the manifesto titled *University or Anti-University* show by a series of examples that these disciplines, particularly the study of literature and philosophy, are occasionally under threat, even though the literary world has never been so much in demand by the economic world, seeking to harness the essential qualities of discernment and judgment. Hence the need, established in a short essay translated into many languages, *The Usefulness of the Useless* (Nuccio Ordine), to promote the teaching of a set of humanistic disciplines capable of encouraging disinterestedness, gratuitousness, a critical spirit (and even more so, postcriticism, as Laurent de Sutter suggests), the "beautiful style," and cultivating our ability, as the writer Annie le Brun puts it, to spot the aesthetics of the parvenu.

For, as Fabien de Gueuser and Alain-Max Guénette point out, management is a novel and the manager, due to the sheer volume of his "literary" productions (speeches, "accounting entries," annual reports, etc.), is also in some way a novelist. It is no coincidence that Zola or Balzac, and more recently Houellebecq, used the business world as the setting for some of their best stories. This should also be seen in the context of the work of philosopher Éric Méchoulan, who shows that the ability to read, men as well as situations, remains an essential quality for a good understanding of social relations.

But that's not all: the quest for all forms of renewal also involves a critique of hubris and gigantism, as Olivier Rey points out in *A question of size*, a concern first raised by the ancient Greeks. Good management means finding the right balance, the right harmony, like Lego, to a certain extent: this is what Tommaso Bertolotti indirectly tries to demonstrate with his enjoyable "Legosophy."

Reflecting on new forms of management also means rethinking possible forms of hospitality, as Michel Agier's essay on contemporary migration encourages us to do. The concern for openness is the condition for the cultural and identity renewal of organizations, and in this spirit I will try to envisage management differently, from the yin and the yang, perhaps to show contemporary managers how to escape contradictions without losing face.

On the Decline of General Culture

Allan Bloom, *The Closing of the American Mind*[18] (New York: Simon & Schuster, 1987).

Exact sciences have taken over our society. Besides, no one thinks of questioning their usefulness; they operate on a principle of military conquest that nothing seems to be able to stop.

However, two points should draw our attention. On the one hand, the fact that the domain of competence of the exact sciences stops short of humanity, which they exclude from their calculations. On the other hand, the observation that they are incapable of informing us on the only question that really matters: What are our values? For what reason do we want to live, work, or even lead collective action? For what reasons do we want to act?

These questions are at the heart of Allan Bloom's famous essay, *The Closing of the American Mind*, in 1987, a book that was not much read in Europe but nevertheless had an immense impact, particularly in the United States. The author explains why and how the humanities give us access to ourselves in a way that is far more authentic than the social sciences, which Bloom criticizes for their lack of unity: "the economy argues that the market economy is the basis of everything," he says, "psychology says that is the individual psyche that underlies everything else, anthropology that it is culture, political science that it is the political order." Everyone wants, he adds, "the story told by the human sciences to be in accordance with their desires and needs" like "those sociologists, who speak so easily of the sacred, and who make one think of a man who has a toothless old circus lion in his house to give him the thrill of the jungle."

The social sciences would thus like to quantify human phenomena while at the same time proving themselves incapable of doing so, because they are above all based on a system of values, of ascribing meaning to the conduct of human actions. Instead, they have installed behaviorism, which pretends with statistics to show how predictable human beings are, thus arguing against all great literature, from Tolstoy to Flaubert. "Literature," says Bloom, "makes me think of the Paris flea market, where among old rubbish and junk goods you can discover a treasure."

This essayist, who died in 1992, wanted to alert his compatriots to the loss of influence of humanist disciplines and even to the risk of their total disappearance within the American university. According to him, it was Europe's honor to have been able to maintain a central place for philosophy, with particular respect for the Socratic figure who symbolizes this curious habit of constantly asking why. He also refers to Nietzschean thought, which constantly reminds us that "victorious rationalism is incapable of reigning" and that leaders are first and foremost, and always have been, those who show themselves capable of generating new ethical and aesthetical perspectives.

Without a "critical heritage," and thus without the ability to differentiate "between the sublime and the junk," the soul appears disarmed, as the French title of this scathing essay indicates. Bloom's tome remains relevant today, primarily for its main thesis, and less so for its categorical and unsuccessful denial of the emergence of poststructuralism in the 1960s and 1970s.

At a time when the use of technology and statistical literacy seem to have replaced humanist culture, in the United States as elsewhere, when "loss of meaning" has become a threatening and recurring theme in the world of work, Bloom's warning, resounding as it is, deserves to be heard more than ever, if not completely believed: "The West is defined in particular by its need for philosophy," he writes. "Deprived of this, it will collapse." Have we taken sufficient account, in our faculties as well as in our ministries, of this transatlantic prediction?

Free Qualities

Pascal Chabot, *Traité des libres qualités*[19] (PUF, 2019).

What is good? What is our idea of good? Presented with such a question, in a classroom for example, very few students take the risk of proffering an answer. We must recognize that this is a difficult question, one that the whole philosophical tradition has had to face. It is, however, an essential point: for then, what would be a good decision? Who could be called a "good person"? What would we mean by the expression "doing her job well"?

For the philosopher Pascal Chabot, the notion of Good seems too often to be summed up nowadays as "what works." If the train arrives on time, that's good. If my computer turns on when I press the on button, that's good, too. However, the question of Good is more about why we want to take transport and why we use our computer, what meaning we give to these actions in relation to the values and ideas that we hold dear and that we wish to defend.

To regain the initiative, in a digital-dataist world that is interested in quantity and how much rather than why, Pascal Chabot proposes a new ethic based not on functionalism or the logic of maxima but on what we might call "qualitarism." An ethic that he sums up in the manner of Kant: "Act in such a way that the quality of life of each being is assured and respected."

The new figure of the Good, says the author, must be that of quality, or rather of free qualities, as the title of this little treatise indicates. These free qualities drive home the point of the author's more general philosophical project, from his essays on global burnout and the age of transitions, which consists in replacing "useful" progress with "subtle" progress, a word derived from the Latin sub-tela, "borrowed from the inspiring imagination of women weavers," which "designates that which lies 'below the surface' of a canvas, i.e. the weave and weft of an embroidered fabric." Without these subtleties, in the end, nothing holds.

For Chabot, there is no doubt that Descartes is the figure in the history of philosophy who did most damage to the standing of qualities. For it was he, along with Locke, who "broke quality down into objective and measurable qualities on the one hand, and subjective and sensitive qualities on the other." First qualities on the one hand, objectifiable, such as the weight of an object; and on the other hand its second qualities, the sensory perception we have of it, its invisible architecture, its value for us. All this to the benefit of the former, always calculable, controllable, while the latter are by nature more difficult to control.

In management, however, a strong temptation still is to want to measure everything, to reduce everything to primary qualities, according to the principle that Peter Drucker established in his time, which holds that what cannot be measured cannot be managed. This is how qualities have been controlled by so-called quality circles since the 1970s, today by systems of standards and norms.

But what about free qualities? Tactfulness, gratuitousness, delicacy, informal benevolence, spirit of finesse . . . not to mention attention to others and care, particularly visible at the time of the emergence of COVID-19, which has shaken up our lifestyles as much as our organizations (starting with the state itself). There can be no doubt that we fail to fully account for all these dimensions, which can hardly be measured in dashboards. And yet, it is these free qualities, which are by no means secondary, that determine the morale of employees and, ultimately, the health of an entire society.

This invitation for managers to become "quality researchers," capable of showing nuance and judgment, Chabot illustrates with an amusing example: it is a little-known fact that the writer-musician Boris Vian was, after his engineering studies at the École Centrale, hired at Afnor, the French Agency for Standardisation, where he stayed for four years. And it was no doubt by dint of setting new standards that Vian, in the evenings, on his way home from the jazz clubs that made him a legend, invented "walls that move, buses that go nowhere, pianocktails and so many other dreams."

Small Treatise on the Great Managerial Virtues

Julien Deonna and Emma Tieffenbach, eds., *Le Petit Traité des valeurs*[20] (Ithaque, 2018).

Management students graduating from higher education define themselves first and foremost, and increasingly, if we take the time to probe their desires, as a collective of women and men motivated by common values and objectives, no longer based on a utilitarian or systemic definition of the company. Consequently, it is highly likely that in the future, it is on this criterion that they will choose to orient themselves, to choose one institution rather than another, one enterprise rather than one of its competitors.

This raises the question of what values their future employer will want to promote. These values already exist, of course, most often tacitly and correspond to beliefs forged over time about the best way to live together within the organization.

However, it should be remembered that the use of the word "value" is always ambiguous. It refers to ideas that are particularly dear to one's heart and that one wishes to defend as a priority, but it also refers to the amount of a property to which a potential investor would have to consent to acquire it. "What is it worth?" is a question open to all interpretations. Values can be translated in many ways and are, therefore, difficult to reconcile into a coherent whole: the values of loyalty and honesty, for example, are sometimes difficult to hold together.

In this *Little Treatise on Values*, intended for a wide audience and produced on the initiative of the members of the department of philosophy of the University of Geneva, we are invited to clarify the meaning we attribute to the aesthetic, political, or moral values we hold dear. For each term—more than twenty of them—one contributor sets out the essential points in a few pages. Let us look more closely at three of these terms, which are particularly rich: interesting, luxury, and solidarity.

Anne Meylan reminds us that "interesting," a word that is constantly heard in companies without necessarily having a clear meaning, first concerns things that are stimulating on a cognitive level and that have a certain relationship with the idea of the good. They must also know how to surprise us, what the author calls the "condition of firstness." She adds another fundamental condition: to be "interesting," something must also be "manageable and graspable." Finally, as research in psychology suggests, interesting is what is placed in the hedonic register: what is interesting is, first and foremost, entertaining, and therefore provides pleasure.

As for luxury, this extraordinarily profitable and fast-growing sector of activity, it would be, first and foremost, this value that concerns unnecessary goods with the character of being ordinary goods: a leather bag, a bottle of wine, a bicycle, for example. Federico Lauria points out that only goods such as "having a degree, having a child, . . . having survived a serious illness or living the perfect love" can be considered extraordinary. Luxury, therefore, appears to be an ordinary good endowed with "extraordinary instances."

Finally, solidarity is a value generally championed within teams above all others. Indeed, it is solidarity that allows us to redeem projects that get off to a bad start, to strengthen bonds even in difficult situations, and to humanize the workplace. However, the entry devoted to solidarity here suggests that we should look twice and always consider, first and foremost, the values that solidarity serves. "The fact that solidarity can serve immoral ends shows us that solidarity actions have no consecutive value," explains Jörg Löschke. "In other words, an action is not good simply because it is carried out of solidarity." To put it even more simply: solidarity between members of criminal networks is certainly not a moral value.

In addition to these three examples, the book makes room for numerous entries shedding light on managerial practice, such as authenticity, power, ownership, and usefulness. And it is also the proof, according to the cheerful expression chosen by the authors, of "the generous diversity that characterises the axiological world."

The Delights of Discreet Successes

David Zweig, *Invisibles: The Power of Anonymous Work in an Age of Relentless Self-Promotion* (London: Penguin, 2014).

Social media, and in particular Facebook, have become immense zones of perpetual self-promotion. Their success is due, in large part, to the competition between users to attract the attention of other users. With participatory media, we are therefore witnessing an unlimited extension of the struggle for recognition in terms of the number of likes—4.5 billion distributed every day on the most popular social network (i.e., for the promotion of oneself as a brand).

Is this search for notoriety essential both to our personal happiness and to our future professional success? David Zweig seems to doubt it vigorously. According to him, the signs of recognition that we obtain through these marketing techniques applied to ourselves do not bring the desired result or satisfaction. These self-promotion techniques put us under the surveillance of others and thus restrict our freedom. Moreover, the author tells us, this need for recognition that we all feel can never be completely fulfilled: it is renewed each time we think we should deserve it, to the point of constituting a claim that is never satisfied, because it is inexhaustible.

Zweig, therefore, contrasts this model with those professionals, heroes we sometimes come across in the workplace without really knowing them, who find in the very exercise of their role a satisfaction that social media are not able to provide. And the author tells us about the astonishing journeys of people we have never heard of, who have no desire for celebrity, yet who, thanks to their know-how, enjoy unparalleled satisfaction.

For example, UN translator Giulia Wilkins Ary, who, thanks to her language skills, enables heads of state who do not speak the same language to get on the same wavelength, even though their interests diverge, and nothing predisposes them to get along. Or Plank, the technician unknown to the general public who has worked on all of Radiohead's gigs for more than twenty years and without whom the band's career would have been very different. Plank, for his part, testifies that his only goal is to bring the band the level of musical technicality it needs and admits that his greatest source of satisfaction is a job well done, a concert that fans will always remember. Similarly, Denis Poon, the chief engineer of the Shanghai Tower, and many other examples, among the soldiers, cooks, or truck drivers who find pride and accomplishment in the exercise of their profession, and especially in proving themselves worthy of the responsibility that has been entrusted to them.

Ultimately, for these "invisible" people, intrinsic motivating factors are far superior to extrinsic motivating factors that they do not care about. Focusing on what they know and what they like to do, they avoid, according to psychologist Sam Gluckberg, quoted in the book, the worries of those who concentrate their efforts on their own self-promotion and lose the energy they need to outperform and innovate in their profession. The book's lesson has a name, eudemony in the classical sense, the idea that well-being is not to be sought in the mirror of others, residing instead in acting for the world and for others, being content with a happiness of living rooted in the meticulous and concrete realization of our capabilities, which we sometimes underestimate.

Interpreting Facts: From Science to Storytelling

John D. Caputo, *Hermeneutics and Information. Facts and Interpretation of the Age of Information* (London: Pelican Book, 2018).

What happens in an organization can always be explained, for some, by the chain of causes and effects, and for others, by the simple presence of stories. This has always been the great fault line among those who have a certain curiosity about management. The former are determined to advance the supposed neutrality of the scientific method, as Taylor did in his time. The latter are determined to decipher the facts of management, to situate them in a broader context, and to derive a sociological, economic, and cultural analysis from them. For the latter in fact, the organization is never a neutral and disinterested space, devoid of all cultural presuppositions. In short, the state of nature in our industrial regions has indeed disappeared.

In his latest book, the American philosopher and theologian John Caputo sets out to show us why this second option is the only credible one. Organizations have no pure and perfectly objective facts: behind accounting statements, strategic options, conflicts between management and employees, or recruitment choices are always contextual elements to be analyzed and decoded. It is all a matter of interpreting the goings on within the company: such is the view advanced by a school of thought ostentatiously called "hermeneutics," of which Caputo is a radical defender.

In Caputo's view, when we believe something, when we try to understand what is happening, all we really are doing is trying to interpret the world. Even mathematics is only one of many ways of deciphering and translating the world.

The company as we think we know it is, therefore, a cultural and mental construct, which would be the best proof that we are not machines. Only human beings are capable of making judgments in specific situations, based on implicit knowledge, certain know-how, or even good manners. As Caputo notes, our machines only know how to calculate, we know how to negotiate, computer programs set up routine operations whereas we are capable of branching off . . . which prompts the author to say that people working in the field of artificial intelligence are not as stupid as the software solutions they put on the market.

But then, what can we say to those who consider that the theory of evolution is a wacky hypothesis, or that the Americans themselves perpetrated the 9/11 attacks? Caputo simply replies that some interpretations are better than others. This is why every decision requires our interpretative capacity, our subtilitas. Every line of reasoning requires our ability to appreciate situations to be as accurate as possible, always remaining "haunted" by the possibility of error.

Whereas management books generally ask us to believe that discipline is essentially programmable, or "predetermined," this essay incites us to look "at the other side," that of "the marginal, the outsider, the surprising, the fortuitous, of everything that comes without our seeing it. The may-being, the perhaps." And Caputo takes the example of medical institutions, especially the work of emergency doctors and nurses, which can inspire managerial practice, to show that their role is not to predict the disasters that are going to happen, which is by definition impossible, but to maintain with vitality their capacity to deal with events that happen without warning.

This useful essay reminds us, against the backdrop of industrial societies increasingly subject to the technological diktat, but nevertheless as fragile as those of the past, as the episodes of lockdown in these two last years have highlighted, of the dual condition of our freedom within organizations: finding the means to form an opinion that belongs only to oneself and retaining a place for the nonprogrammable within institutions. This is the only way we can maintain the possibility of renewing ourselves and, why not, truly innovating.

Is Teaching the Humanities Still Useful?

Paolo Quintili, Carlo Cappa, and Donatella Palomba, *Université ou anti-Université. Les humanités dans l'idée de formation supérieure*[21] (L'Harmattan, 2016).

"Rather than deepening highly theoretical university research, we encourage more technical and professional education that better anticipates the needs of society." These words, spoken by former Japanese Prime Minister Shinzo Abe, leave little doubt as to his opinion of the study of literature, history, and philosophy. Following this statement, the initiative was taken to abolish many humanities departments in the country. According to an adviser to the minister, "students should first learn to use accounting software rather than read the texts of economist Paul Samuelson, and learn English-Japanese translation useful for explanations to tourists rather than Shakespeare."

This little Japanese story, reported by Jacques Derrida's translator into Japanese, Yuji Nishiyama, illustrates the extreme frailty of literary teachings in the face of power and society. Indeed, in the minds of many, well beyond the political elites of Tokyo, literary and philosophical studies are useless in the face of technological progress, as evidenced by the near nullity of their use value on the labor market.

This judgment is not only wrong but also very dangerous. It would be very unwise to give it any credit at all. False, indeed: never before have the humanities been of such precious use in training citizens and responsible actors. As the authors of this collective work point out, these disciplines are irreplaceable in fostering, among other things, ethical and aesthetic sensitivity, written and oral communication between people from different cultures, the intellectual enlightenment of the future voters that we are—in short, the autonomy of thought of every one of us. To understand the future, we need a humanity that is curious and open-minded, and the humanities play a key role in this.

American elites, too rapidly accused by some Europeans of lacking culture, have understood this much better than them: in world-renowned institutions such as Harvard, MIT, and Stanford, where fifteen departments in the humanities coexist, the liberal arts are at the heart of the educational system. In England, a study shows that more than a third of the companies in the "FTSE 100" are run by graduates of the humanities and social sciences. In France, an article published in cadreemploi.fr on the class of 2018 graduates bore the unequivocal title: "The human sciences are a hit," adding, "As last year, graduates in human and social sciences are the most numerous in finding work, with a record employment rate of 88% one year after their arrival on the job market."[22]

Those who still advocate the gradual abandonment of the humanities at school are naive at best: as the computer-led economy continues to expand its reach, driven by artificial intelligence that anticipates our own desires, we need to be able to take back the initiative and think for ourselves.

Hannah Arendt famously noted that a cultured person was, first and foremost, someone who knew how to "choose his companions from among men, things and thoughts, in the present as in the past," suggesting that philosophical knowledge serves, first and foremost, to identify talents, to create bonds of trust with others, and to separate the wheat from the chaff in so-called new ideas—three aptitudes that are clearly essential in the management of organizations.

It is important, however, as Derrida himself reminded us, "not to allow ourselves to be trapped inside the humanities." The "soft sciences" would, therefore, be well advised to open up to other practices where "the exercise of thought" takes place, such as management, industry, or marketing. Such meeting places exist, such as the Collège International de Philosophie, which Derrida cofounded in 1983 and was the driving force behind this book.

The Indispensable Utility of the Useless

Nuccio Ordine, *The Usefulness of the Useless* (Paul Dry Books, 2017).

If we had to define the dominant philosophy of our time, we would have little difficulty in agreeing on the preeminence of utilitarianism. This doctrine of political philosophy extends its influence across all continents, embracing governments with very different or even opposing political options, and even in small or large organizations: the morality of an action is evaluated according to its effects, thus always proceeding from the point of view of utility. This is called payoff in the United States, or ROI (i.e., return on investment). But is utility only concerned with what pays off? And should we equate what is useful with what is profitable?

Nuccio Ordine seems to have great doubts about this: on the one hand, we must find room for uselessness to exist in our world dominated by utilitarianism; and on the other hand, we must recognize its share of utility. With this mischievous title, this Italian literary critic, a specialist of Giordano Bruno and the Renaissance, proposes a challenge to the reign of utility. Indeed, as he tells us in passing, the useless characterizes humanity at least as much as the useful: the sciences, the arts, all forms of intellectual and spiritual curiosity are not necessarily based on a principle of efficiency, and this is precisely what gives them their importance, indeed it is the prerogative and privilege of the human being. To be human is, first, to know how to recognize the usefulness of the useless. Perhaps, in the register of useful things, indeed the useless should be placed first. Hence the importance, the author warns, of not "gradually killing" in our educational system "the memory of the past, humanistic disciplines, classical languages, instruction, free research, fantasy, art, critical thinking."

This little book is important—useful even—for the economic world, providing two opportunities for reflection.

Before being useful to systems, some of the work experience of managers will always escape the principle of usefulness. The satisfaction of completing a project, the experienced mutual support between team members, the frustrations they will experience during their assignments sometimes—all this will be experienced beyond the immediately measurable, calculable, and profitable. Something in the systems that promotes utility escapes them.

Hence the second benefit to be drawn from this work: what escapes the systems is precisely the force of uselessness; that is to say, deep down, the hidden meaning of utility, its humanism. Ordine quotes a 1961 lecture by Eugène Ionesco:

> Look at the busy people in the streets. . . . They go straight ahead, but always without looking in front of them, because they can complete their journey, which they know in advance, mechanically. . . . The man in a hurry doesn't understand that, in the end, it's the useful that can be a useless, overwhelming weight. If one does not understand the usefulness of the useless, the uselessness of the useful, one does not understand art; and a country where one does not understand art is a country of slaves or robots, . . . a country without spirit.

Understanding art to avoid acting like a machine is a prerequisite that managers, in the age of artificial intelligence, which will soon compete with them in many aspects of their job (especially in monitoring and control), will have to take into account.

This little book, which also takes in Baudelaire's criticism of the useful man, Italo Calvino's praise of gratuitousness, Kant's disinterested judgment of taste, and Victor Hugo's campaign for an increase in the culture budget, allows us to better appreciate the different meanings of the word "useful"—in short, to distinguish the essential from the accessory.

For behind this cry for humanist culture hardly hides a criticism of educational projects that tend to exclude grace, beauty, and spirit from their programs. As Ordine has it, we must finally consider "as useful everything that helps us to become better."

Postcriticism

Laurent de Sutter, ed., *Postcritique* (PUF, 2019).

Outside economic circles, it is easy to imagine that management studies remain above all at the service of the industrial machine and not a place for critical discussion. However, the opposite is more than likely: management, as a practice, as a form of learning, or as a scientific research interest, is resolutely intended to be a place for critical reflection in an attempt to renew management practice, learning, and research in search of greater efficiency, fairness, or justice.

To this last point critical management studies, which have been developed throughout the world since the early 1990s and rely on philosophers such as Michel Foucault or Jacques Derrida to explore the limits and aporias of classical management techniques, are particularly devoted. They have made it possible to denounce some of the absurdities and injustices of organizational life.

In management, criticizing usually means revealing the concrete conditions of operations, the duplicity or incoherence of certain discourses, the lack of ethical and political sensitivity of so-called good practices and fashionable technological tools. It is quite simply a question of bringing to light what is really going on in organizations without being satisfied with the smoke screens sometimes created by the rather poor language palette of management.

But is it not now time to turn criticism on its head, to be surprised to see this discourse becoming institutionalized, in the same way as those it claims to fight? Has this school of thought developed a belief in systematic negation, an assumption that criticism must necessarily be negative? In short, has critical thinking not become in the human and social sciences—as there are critical legal studies in law, for example—a somewhat too comfortable way of asserting rather than doubting, of excommunicating rather than sharing, of judging the world rather than trying to transform it?

These questions are at the heart of an important text by Bruno Latour published in the *Critical Inquiry*, available online,[23] which already asked the question, "Why has critique run out of steam?" Why does critique have nothing more to say, except to deconstruct an economic, social, and environmental world in need of rebuilding? It is in the direction of this theoretical clarification that a dozen philosophers have come together under the direction of Laurent de Sutter to propose an alternative that they call postcriticism.

It is not a question here of criticizing criticism in the form of an endless negative spiral, but of trying to stand beside it, or behind it, to give it back its active and affirmative power. One of the contributors, Dorian Astor, evokes Nietzsche's amor fati (love of destiny), "that philosophy that never stops saying yes after every no, behind every no." Far from the aggressiveness, certainty, and arrogance of criticism, Astor emphasizes the "gracious and loving kindness of postcritical perspectivism." In short, this a question of thinking not against but for, in the manner proposed by Pacôme Thiellement, another contributor here, who argues that for too long criticizing has meant disliking, isolating, classifying, cataloging, and in the end, judging. Critics, he argues, "spend less time liking what they like than disliking what they don't like." But they might as well spend that time questioning the basis of their attractions rather than the reasons for their anger or resentment.

What can we learn from all this as we think about management? In the end, it is not a question of opposing a presumptuous, or even contemptuous, discourse in response to managerial Newspeak, which sometimes proves to be empty of meaning indeed, as the critical school already does; but rather, as De Sutter himself proposes, to try to "narrate instead of judging" and to "accept weakness instead of claiming strength."[24]

To borrow another of his formulations, we could take up again regarding management what he himself says about the law: before criticizing management, we must begin by accepting the idea that management exists and that this has been the case for ages. And that this managerial reality should not be confused with politics, or with economics, or with sociology, even the sociology of organizations. There is management, and this management "is nothing more than what we do with it."

Advantage, therefore, to post-management practitioners, enlightened by a philosophy more concerned with transformative and creative influence than with critical conformity.

Industrial Design or "Parvenu Aesthetics"?

Annie Le Brun, *Ce qui n'a pas de prix*[25] (Stock, 2018).

"Ugliness sells poorly." Raymond Loewy, the founder of industrial design, seems to be stating the obvious with this maxim, which provided the title for one of his books. Without a constant effort to make products more attractive for those who design and promote them, they are ugly and do not sell well. The aesthetic equation is a requirement of the times.

Yet Annie Le Brun does not seem convinced, to say the least, by the saturation effects of our sensibilities imposed by the permanent recourse to the massive aesthetics represented by contemporary design. All you need to do is "venture into the maze of one of the countless magazines aimed at children," she says, "to be seized by the coarseness of shapes and colours as well as the vulgarity of the materials."

It must be said that for Annie Le Brun, a literary critic who has remained faithful to the surrealist movement and a specialist on the Marquis de Sade, whose work she presented at the Musée d'Orsay, we are increasingly enclosed in spaces where there are too many objects and too many images—as she puts it, "signifiers without signified." So much so, she jokes, that "it is no longer beings but selfies who travel." Our capacity for wonder as well as our faculties of analysis are thus left to languish: "the transition from quantity to quality is no longer made," "domination no longer claims to be a system of values but prescribes a way of being determined by the indifference of numbers." The result is that we are no longer sensitive to anything, deprived of our emotional capacities, as a result, more often than not, of gigantism. She illustrates this with China, which will soon be offering Trier, Marx's birthplace, a five-meter-high statue of the German intellectual on the pretext "that a great philosopher needs a great statue!"

According to the author, the relationship between the business world and the art world has played a role in this evolution. Contemporary artists with a worldwide reputation, such as Anish Kapoor or Jeff Koons, have become managers, not doing their own work as artists but delegating it and responding to commissions from wealthy people. They also act as industrial investors, Kapoor thus appropriating absolute black, the "Vantablack," which has the particularity of capturing almost all light and only the artist can now use in his works. For Le Brun, the result is a sort of "parvenu aesthetics," which by its very omnipresence and immoderation is robbing us of our inner world, at the instigation of an art market finally monopolized by a few artists, always the same ones, and a handful of billionaire benefactors or patrons of the arts, all in the name of a global cosmeticization of the outside world that we can no longer avoid.

The author's response is that we should go back to searching for what is "priceless." To resist at all costs to the "liquidation of the night of the incalculable," according to her beautiful expression, is to resist this threatening evolution of contemporary art.

In organizations, the question of beauty can by no means be reduced to placing a few reproductions of paintings in the corridors leading to the meeting room, where the rest of the series awaits us. On the other hand, the task of a management that is sensitive to the aesthetic question is to ask itself first what beauty can do to effectively transform working relationships.

We could argue that the notion of a beau geste,[26] rather than empty words that are often derisory in scope, should attract the attention of managers. By questioning the standards and practices they institute, beautiful gestures bring about a far more radical transformation than upgrading the company's design furniture and offices to the aesthetic standards of the age, whatever the cost.

The Stories We Tell

Fabien de Geuser and Alain Max Guénette, eds., *Littérature et management : Le management comme roman et le manager comme romancier?*[27] (L'Harmattan, 2018).

Should the field of management be situated on the side of cause and effect, as the mechanistic view of management holds, or on the side of the interpretation of organizational facts in the sense that, as Jean-Pierre Dupuy reminds us,[28] quoting Adam Smith, the economy is only a vast theater stage "where society tells stories about itself?"

With this collective work, Fabien de Geuser and Alain Max Guénette opt decisively for the second option. Organizations cannot be reduced to a set of configurable objects. They also point out that the manager is the author of texts, statements, speeches, of course—we even talk about "accounting writing" or "ledgers." They show us that the manager is also the chief reader of the organizations for which she is responsible, through the reports, accounts, and strategic analyses that she reads. Finally, they show that, like writers and playwrights, the entrepreneur is someone who creates. Bergson is remembered for explaining that the joy of the entrepreneur who has created her business is akin to that of "the artist who has realised her thought or the scientist who has discovered or invented." The management choices would be, in a way, "auctorial" gestures, behind which one or more authors sign the action undertaken. The actors, the managers themselves, are not always fully aware of all this. It is the aim of this book to help us understand to what extent business life is, first and foremost, made up of dramatic events, of more or less colorful characters, of failed or successful interpretations, of effective or failed staging, of deep or superficial narratives.

In this timely book, we move from the study of novels that put businesses at the heart of their stories, from Zola to Houellebecq, to the analysis of management situations in various literary genres: Balzac and the misfortunes of the perfumer César Birotteau; Victor Hugo inventing in Jean Valjean a figure of social boss, secret philanthropist, and recurring paternalist. Molière, in the theater, turns his bourgeois nobleman into a character who imagines himself to be loved for who he is, a small boss incapable of self-mockery, driven by his impulses and always ready to take the path of imitation, as Denis Malherbe and Laurence Kauffman note in passing, making a connection with Di Maggio and Powell's theories on organizational isomorphism, a strategy of full conformity with a competing model that gives their zealots the impression of being original.

Among the contributors here is James Marsh, one of the most influential authors in contemporary management studies, who for the past few years has devoted himself to the analysis of major literary texts to better understand leadership issues. Marsh finds, for example, in Ibsen and his *Wild Duck* the reasons why we generally accredit myths that, on a rational level, we should challenge. Here he quotes Dr. Relling, one of the main characters in the play, who shows how "illusions must be encouraged as the lies necessary for life. Take away their hopes of success and you take away their ability to be happy." Cervantes's willful blindness also provides Marsh with an opportunity to illustrate his thesis that leadership is a matter of passions rather than reason.

The book is interspersed with numerous half-managerial, half-literary analyses, such as the one reported by a former student explaining why the reading of Jules Romain's *Men of Good Will* inspired her more than the resolution of the Pur Soup and Philishave business cases.

All in all, this is a noteworthy book, which demonstrates that literature about organizations can sometimes breathe new life into literature and always brings something new to the way we look at organizations.

Reading, Learning, Leading

Éric Méchoulan, *Lire avec soin. Amitié, justice et médias*[29] (ENS Éditions, 2017).

In Liberté et Patrie, Jean-Luc Godard tells this story:

> "Father, what is the best way to find out if someone is worth dating?"
>
> "You have to ask him: what have you read? And if he answers you: Homer, Shakespeare, Balzac, the man is not fit for company. If, on the other hand, he answers you: what do you mean by reading? Then there is room for hope."

This bon mot of the most capricious of the New Wave filmmakers raises questions about the importance we attribute in social and professional life to the act of reading: Is it indeed a matter, when we read, of accumulating data on literary history? If this were the case, it is highly likely that literary culture would continue to be omitted from list of strengths required of those in positions of responsibility, especially in the corporate world.

But if reading means first questioning the deep meaning of words and situations, showing sound judgment and skills, even refinement in human affairs, then it is quite different: knowing how to read becomes the only skill that can enlighten all the others. So much so that we might think that the absence of learning to read attentively in the training of individuals, and especially managers, who have become bad company, as Godard indicates, might be considered a matter of prime educational concern.

First, we should perhaps try to answer the second question suggested by the filmmaker: "What do we mean by reading?" It is to this question that Éric Méchoulan addresses himself, considering the activity of reading from the written media, naturally placed at the center of the game, to better extend its general meaning and show that we never stop reading and being read. Social and professional life can be described as a book in which the characters (us) are constantly being recognized, described, or judged, with the difference that these characters are themselves readers of the situations in which they are embarked. In other words, all social behavior of any kind is always the result of our reading the stories of which we are partly the authors, while at the same time we try to "make ourselves readable." As the Canadian philosopher Charles Taylor rightly points out, all sociability implies that we are "able to 'read' each other."

This point of view thus sheds light on the activity of reading in a slightly different light from that to which literature courses have accustomed us: rather than a more or less sophisticated form of entertainment, reading is first of all a tool for deciphering social relations in the service of our own existence. As Hobbes put it, "Wisdom is acquired not by reading books, but by reading people." Books are a way of interpreting the world, a necessary tool, not in the interests of literature but of the way we live in society. For if it is important to know how to read, it is first to better understand the worlds in which we are involved and the people that, in such circumstances, we are constantly encountering.

This is why the subtitle of the book refers to the media, which may be surprising at first glance. "Paying attention to the media," writes the author, "is precisely about exploring the various ways in which they produce that 'in-between.'" Using social media such as Twitter and Facebook is a matter of making oneself accessible and intelligible to others. "Reading is always an exchange": another way of expressing the idea that to read or make oneself readable, in turn, is to engage in a discussion whose aim should be to enable everyone to see the world with greater precision and nuance. Hence the importance of choosing one's medium carefully before being read: Descartes, for example, of whom Méchoulan is a specialist, duly chose his message according to the literary genres at his disposal, "discourse, treatise, principles, meditations, etc." His *Discourse on the Method* was written in French and not in Latin, to make it accessible to a nonspecialist audience.

Expressing yourself in writing today offers many more possibilities. A new concept in organizations studies or philosophy will first be presented in peer-reviewed conferences and scientific articles, then in the form of books and press articles before being popularized, for example, on Dailymotion or LinkedIn. But before this approach can take on its full meaning, we must first learn to read. Because, as Charles Péguy put it in his own style, "teaching to read, that is the only true end of teaching, of course: if the reader knows how to read, all is saved."[30]

The Right Strategy Is a Matter of Size

Olivier Rey, Une question de taille[31] (Stock, 2014).

What if all organizational problems ultimately boiled down to one issue: Size? Not inefficiency, as Taylor thought; not motivation, as the theorists of the school of human relations imagined, but the right proportion. To manage an organization well, wouldn't it be above all to give it its ideal size, its optimal balance? This point was essential for a largely forgotten theorist, Leopold Kohr, as Olivier Rey reminds us here. For Kohr, indeed,

> There seems to be only one cause behind all forms of social misery: excessive size. . . . Excessive size appears to be the one and only problem permeating all creation. Wherever something goes wrong, something is too big.

This proposal seems to reduce all the problems of social life somewhat abruptly to questions of proportion. But it must be noted that in the time of the ancient Greeks, as we see in the Philebe, a Socratic dialogue, the first good to be considered in all things was that of measure, the metron. And it is based on this criterion that we can then agree on everything else: the truth of science, beauty, pleasures, and so forth, everything is subject to the condition of good proportion. Not the quantitative measurements that increasingly inform the decision making of companies but, rather, the right measure, which describes an ability to find the right dosage, the right balance, to show also a sense of opportunity—the well-known kairos.

To better understand the nuance, Olivier Rey evokes the old palace that Ceaucescu had built in Bucharest and could be said to be perfectly symmetrical. But for the author, a philosopher as well as a mathematician, this definition of equilibrium, "the invariance of an object through certain mathematical transformations," is the exact opposite of equilibrium in the sense of the Greeks, who first sought grace and concordance between the parts.

This is a way of reconciling us, if not with governance by numbers, then at least with the possibility of harmonious relationship between quality and quantity. For a company, this does not mean growth at all costs—we won't mention the names Vivendi Universal or AOL Time Warner, so as not to bring back bad memories to anyone—but finding the maximum threshold for any extension. It also means that the debates on growth and decline, which occupy so many economists of all stripes, are no longer really relevant, because it is, above all, a question of finding the right balance and sticking to it: growth when the company needs to grow to find its balance, degrowth when it brings with it more problems and a disproportionate increase in the means required to resolve them.

Behind all this, there is an obsession shared by the Greeks and many academic works on mergers and acquisitions have highlighted: the hubris of managers, their occasional incapacity to conduct human affairs with moderation.

This criticism of gigantism and limitlessness has the merit of bringing us back down to earth without totally taking us out of globalization. It also shows that in business management, symmetry is perhaps better than synergy.

The Art of Assembling Bricks

Tommaso Bertolotti, *Legosophie. Petite philosophie du Lego*[32] (PUF, 2019).

We are in the fifth century BC, in the presence of the divine Socrates. Against all odds, he is questioned by a certain Kritoboulos about the difference between a bad and a good manager. It must be said that this question, which is certainly a very judicious one and whose correct answer is not as simple as it seems, had never been asked before. It is, therefore, a great first, long before Fayol and Taylor, twenty-five centuries later, asked it again. Here is what Socrates answers, as related by Xenophon:

> Well, Kritoboulos, if I let you see first of all people who build inconvenient houses at great expense, and then others who, spending much less, build houses with all the desirable comforts, don't you think that in this I will show you what "management" is all about?

Socrates thus makes management a way of building intelligently and efficiently, much like Lego—incidentally, a brand name that apparently has more reach than Google, Nike, or Ferrari (according to a study quoted by Brand Finance). The philosopher here becomes a "Legosopher." A Lego philosophy is precisely what Tommaso Bertolotti proposes in this short essay, which at first glance appears to be a kind of "Legographic" archaeology.

Lego models, the author claims, are "specifically Platonic. Why is that? Because of a very strong relationship with the idea of good, the importance of the model itself, the mathematical dimension, the way in which the builder constructs Lego by looking at the model." Indeed, Plato, Socrates's pupil, was attached to the social harmony in which each person found her place, or a function, that corresponded to her aptitudes. These building bricks, made in Denmark from a single material (acrylonitrile butadiene styrene), allow us not only to understand Platonic concepts but also to implement the principles of management according to Socrates: taking into account the constraints of the system—Lego's studs and holes—and the resources available to build an almost perfect world where everyone, plumber and policeman, hero and thief, would have their places assigned and where there would be an "equal dignity of tasks."

Lego invites us to "build the world," learning that entities only make sense when they are put together, ordered in relation to each other, associated to form a universe, a unique and irreplaceable organization like no other. The toy then functions as a tool for conceptualization, innovation, and development, words that undoubtedly belong to the managerial vocabulary. These embedded forms would be an opportunity for players to think about problem solving based not only on preparatory thinking, but also on the manipulation of objects. And it is here that we must remember, once again, that the word management comes from the Latin manus, the hand.

And yet the metaphor finds its limits where the relevance of the comparison breaks down, like two bricks that cannot finally be put together, contrary to the instructions for use. The blissful and ultimately inexplicable faces of our figurines, capable of showing only one emotion, a false indifference at most, intrigue Bertolotti. These gloomy faces indicate a kind of paralysis, a despondency, a form of depression as well. Problems all too familiar in the working world: Is Lego, in fact, a perfect illustration of the phenomena of burnout or bore-out? An example of what not to do?

Nevertheless, there is a strong lesson here for organizations: the founder of the concept, Ole Kirk Christiensen, found the name Lego from the Danish expression "leg godt," which means "play well." This is precisely what companies need to rediscover today, by giving everyone the opportunity to change functions, to express themselves fully and, above all, to get out of the state of immobility where our managerial concepts of another century seem to have frozen us.

Rethinking Hospitality in Contemporary Organizations

Michel Agier, *L'étranger qui vient. Repenser l'hospitalité*[33] (Seuil, 2018).

Migration is a phenomenon that every nation has a duty to consider. And it must be noted that it is often the yardstick by which membership of a political camp is determined, at least in Western nations. Today, the "migrant crisis," as it is a bit hastily called, largely structures our social debates.

This is not surprising, according to Michel Agier, anthropologist and director of studies at EHESS,[34] for whom much of who we are is determined by our understanding of otherness. According to him, this understanding is informed by four primordial motivations: the suffering to which we are exposed and we feel is intolerable, its similarity to us, its difference—which the author calls the "exotic cause"—and finally the heroic status that we confer on it and legitimizes the support that we must give it.

The author begins by pointing out that a world without hospitality would by definition be unlivable, because it is precisely in confrontation with the other, the different, that our societies move and develop. Nevertheless, and nuance is everything here, the author has no intention of burying his head in the sand: the foreigner, the migrant, is always an intruder. "We find this meaning in the English foreigner," explains Agier, "and also in the Spanish forastero or the French forain: in old French, the forain is 'the stranger in the village.'" English is particularly enlightening here, a language in which the word host is derived from the French for guest, while the word hostage means prisoner. The one who receives is also the prisoner of the one she receives, the relationship between the two always being asymmetrical. Maybe hospitality is finally not an "egalitarian" gift: we can see this through the testimonies that the author evokes concerning the "burn-out of the humanitarians," the "over-investment of the hosts" or the "fatigue of the hosted."

This essay is by no means a treatise on well-meaning sentiments, seeking instead to reexamine the dynamics of obligation, the sense of testing that is always a key part of hospitality. Hospitality can also be understood as hostility: precisely in an attempt to break out of this ambivalence, and this impasse, the German philosopher Immanuel Kant formulated his *Project for Perpetual Peace* in 1795. The idea was to acknowledge the fact that our world being round, world citizenship, cosmopolitanism, and ultimately the cessation of hostilities, inevitably implied a right to move from one country to another; that this right was necessarily the condition for peace, and for economic and cultural development.

Yet, writes Agier, it is clear today that "the Mediterranean, the Mexican desert, the Sahara and the Bay of Bengal have become tombs of this universalism." And the author invites us, rather, perhaps in a more realistic way, to meditate on this "pure intelligence of the world," in Etienne Tassin's words, which ultimately defines the principle of hospitality.

This intelligence is still required at the level of states as well as organizations. Wouldn't making organizations more "hospitable," for many of them, so that they are more civilized and therefore, more humane, be a noble objective? Because the same also applies to businesses, whose organizational character is nothing more than the transgression of previous identities, as Olivier Babeau and Jean-François Chanlat's work on innovation has clearly shown:[35] the place they give to those who come to strengthen the group by their presence is an expression of corporate culture, which can be closed or, in the interests of renewal and revitalization, more open.

Yin-Yang: Thinking and Managing Differently

Cyrille J. D. Javary, *Yin Yang. La Dynamique du monde*[36] (Albin Michel, 2018).

The profession of manager is often associated with an exercise that is contrary to the game of "neither yes nor no." To be a manager would mean, several times a day and continuously, knowing how and when to say yes or no. Indecision is not considered to be a managerial virtue: not knowing how to say yes or no is a form of indeterminacy and therefore, a lack of character.

And yet, is this not a very Western vision of things? In China, a good manager, on the contrary, will be the one who never says yes or no, but who, on the contrary, knows how to bring together these oppositions, these contradictions, to overcome them. This principle is well known as yin and yang.

But the very fact that we use the conjunction and between yin and yang immediately reveals our inability to understand this other way of reasoning. In Chinese, in fact, it is common to think in pairs, yin-yang being most often a single word, as in the expression "sweet-sour." Each term expresses not a state but a tendency, an orientation, an inclination, a passing state. If "soft" and "suppleness" are consonant with yin, it is because the yin-like effect is "to soften." In echo, if "firm" and "firmness" are related to yang, it's because the yang-type effect is to "firm up," explains Cyrille Javary, author of this book.

The yin-yang perspective is a great way to denounce false dualisms, to highlight the dynamism of living things, made of continuous changes. Bruce Lee used the image of bicycle pedals to show that the cyclist moves forward if and only if one foot goes up when the other goes down in a harmonious, rhythmic manner. In this way, day is not opposed to night but depends on it. This is why the "heavy/light" opposition does not work in Chinese because it seems to describe two states, whereas in the yin-yang perspective, it only describes two tendencies, one to load, the other to unload.

The book illustrates this alternative way of thinking using examples known to Westerners: the Great Wall, for example, was designed both as a line of defense to prevent the enemy's advance and as a place of communication with the outside world. Javary, without pretending to ignore the atrocities of Maoism, also recalls the elements that make the so-called Great Helmsman a follower of yin-yang. Indeed, he considered that every problem is made up of a primordial contradiction and a second one, one taking the place of the other and vice versa. Mao thus did not hesitate to reverse the order of priorities, this great shift that the *I Ching*, the book that dates back to the origin of Chinese writing, calls the "mutant line." When it was necessary, Mao allied with the internal enemy, to expel the Japanese, for example, before then, but only then, resuming the struggle for central power in China.

This skillful balancing act contains several lessons that may help us to better understand the Chinese business world: first, we must understand that change is the only immutable and constant factor; everything else is subject to continuous transformation, and strategy in particular, which imposes successive moments of conquest and others of retreat. We must then stop lamenting unnecessarily in the face of interlocutors who, not knowing how to say yes or no on principle, are most concerned with ensuring that you do not lose face, nor do they.

All in all, what the Chinese are looking for is not a principle of truth but a principle of efficiency: it is a question of escaping the contradictions that leave us paralyzed and unable to act. To move beyond such obstructions, Chinese literary and philosophical culture invites us to consider how our inconsistencies, our crises, and our misunderstandings are also the ideal moments in which to transform things, both inside and outside ourselves.

NOTES

1. See Pascal Chabot, *Global Burn-Out* (Paris: PUF, 2013).
2. *The Revolt of the Class Leaders.* Crappy jobs, search for meaning, and urban reconversions.
3. André Gorz, *Métamorphoses du travail : quête du sens* (Paris: Galilée, 1988), 141–42.
4. *Postcritical Management Studies* (Dordrecht: Springer, 2023).
5. Market meditations.
6. Georges Bataille, "La notion de dépense," in *La Part maudite* (Paris: Minuit, 2014), 23–24.
7. From the name of the author of a book that is often cited as a reference in marketing learning.
8. *Psychoanalysis of organizations. Theory, clinic, interventions.*
9. *Humanist companies: how they will change the world.*
10. M. McLuhan, *Pour comprendre les médias* (Paris: Seuil, 1968), 88.
11. *Someone to talk to. A History of the Inner Voice.*
12. French National Institute of Health and Medical Research.
13. *Liberty. The power to create.*
14. Talent in debate.

15. P. Bourdieu, *Les Règles de l'art* (Paris: Seuil, 1992), 162.

16. *The Future of Interiority in the Age of New Technologies.*

17. *The (French) National Centre for Scientific Research.*

18. Published in French: L'Âme désarmée. Essai sur le déclin de la culture générale (Les Belles Lettres, 2019).

19. *Treatise on free qualities.*

20. *The Little Treatise on Values.*

21. *University or anti-university. Humanities in higher education*

22. Cécile Husetowski, "Les sciences humaines font un carton," https://www.cadremploi.fr/editorial/actualites/actu-emploi/detail/article/jeunes-diplomes-2018-ceux-qui-decrocheront-un-emploi-facilement-et-les-autres.html.

23. http://www.bruno-latour.fr/sites/default/files/89-CRITICAL-INQUIRY-GB.pdf.

24. It would be interesting to develop a parallel here with the notion of "weak management"; see G. Deslandes, "Weak Theology and Organization Studies," *Organization Studies 41*, no. 1 (2018): 127–39.

25. *Priceless.*

26. J.-P. Bouilloud and G. Deslandes, "The Aesthetics of Leadership: Beau Geste as Critical Behaviour," *Organization Studies*, 2015.

27. *Literature and Management: management as novel and the manager as novelist?*

28. J. P. Dupuy, *L'Avenir de l'économie. Sortir de l'écomystification* (Paris: Flammarion, 2012).

29. *Read with care. Friendship, justice and media.*

30. Charles Péguy, *Pensées*, 1934, in *Œuvres complètes,* tome 1 (Paris: Gallimard, "Bibliothèque de la Pléiade," 1986), 1103.

31. *A question of size.*

32. *Legosophie.* Little Lego philosophy.

33. *The foreigner who comes. Rethinking hospitality.*

34. The School for Advanced Studies in the Social Sciences (based in Paris).

35. O. Babeau and J.-F. Chanlat, "La transgression, une dimension oubliée de l'organisation," *Revue française de gestion 183*, no. 3 (2008): 201–19, doi: 10.3166/rfg.183.201-219.

36. *Yin Yang. The dynamics of the world.*

Conclusion

"From Text to Action"?

> It is not in Montaigne, but in myself, that I find all that I see in him. —Blaise Pascal, *Thoughts*, 1670.

For Pascal, reading is an exercise like no other. Its real fruitfulness lies in discovering within ourselves ("finding" within ourselves) what others know ("seeing" what Montaigne was able to write), and thus revisiting our affects to transform the world as well as ourselves. The practice of reading-as-revealing can therefore be understood in two interconnected ways: on the one hand, opening our ears to a discourse that is capable of transforming us; and, on the other, recognizing truths that we have carried in a latent state without having been able to "find" them by ourselves.

HERMENEUTICS AND ORGANIZATIONS

In an economic world undergoing constant and dramatic technological, geopolitical and ecological change, where no single decision maker can master all the parameters, reading is a more powerful tool for discovery and learning than any other. First because it allows us to familiarize ourselves with issues discussed by authors who take it upon themselves to give us a "glimpse" of the risks and opportunities that the future holds. But, and above all, reading these texts and essays in the human and social sciences, through the interpretative divergences that they reveal, and through the conversation that takes place in the background between them, can help us to better navigate our way through life (by actively appropriating and reconfiguring meaning, especially in the strategic and ethical spheres). This implies active appropriation on the part of the reader and, consequently, the reconfiguration of meaning. This is the hermeneutic horizon of reading for economic decision makers: to question oneself to understand oneself better and, ultimately, to act better.[1] This self-questioning corresponds precisely to the need highlighted in the introduction and business education is supposed to address: to transform the managerial profession to make it better, more open, more hospitable, and more noble. Or to put it another way, more subtle. This term voluntarily invokes Gadamer's use of Rambach's differentiation between the three subtilitas involved in the art of interpretation: subtilitas intelligendi, subtilitas explicandi and subtilitas applicandi, which are based on the notions of understanding, explanation, and application.[2]

It is at the intersection of the world referred to by the text and the world belonging to the reader's own world that a better understanding of oneself and the world emerges for the reader. The world referred to by the text, the "world of the text" to use Ricoeur's expression, is the horizon of possibility opened up by the reading experience, the opportunity for the reader to recapture, or rediscover, a second "naiveté," whereby subjectivity is put on hold, enabling her to project herself into the action once again. A human "action"—in this case, managerial action— in turn, falls into the category of text in the sense that it is susceptible to operations of comprehension and interpretation.[3] It is as if, for Ricoeur, the becoming-action of the text evolves into the becoming-text of action, in a circular movement.

With Ricoeur, and his notion of "second naiveté," the postcritical presupposition of hermeneutics appears most clearly. The philosopher who wrote the famous *Conflict of Interpretations* situates his approach at the crossroads of productive dissonances, at the heart of rival interpretations, suspicious on the one hand (Marx, Freud, Nietzsche) and trusting (or naive) on the other. Ricoeur does not seek to overcome this hermeneutical rivalry but, rather, to bring together the most relevant perspectives, indulging neither the pre-critical credulity nor the absolute incredulity that is supposed to be the hallmark of the "critical" schools, whose common denominators Felski describes as "a spirit of skeptical questioning or outright condemnation, an emphasis on its precarious position vis-à-vis overbearing and oppressive social forces, the claim to be engaged in some kind of radical intellectual and/or political work, and the assumption that whatever is not critical must therefore be uncritical."[4]

In short, if we want the interpretive exercise to be productive, we need to strip away as much dogma as possible. In the selection of researchers and essayists in the humanities and social sciences included here, a large number seem to be better at saying no than yes and can be associated with the suspicious trend. But it would be a mistake to ignore the fact that there are other possible approaches, where moods are expressed differently, and methods also differ. Admittedly, in both cases their approaches are sometimes open to criticism, and I have not hesitated to point this out; but on the other hand, their coexistence seems to me to be productive in that it expands the reach of these texts and serves as a call to action for readers. Readers then participate in a process that, for Gadamer, remains the very definition of hermeneutics and consists in recognizing that "it is perhaps the other who is right."[5] It is not so much the "objective" content that is important in the act of reading—as a Kierkegaardian hermeneutic, for instance, would have us believe—but the ability to listen to the speaker in his/her very subjective gesture of addressing me.

TOWARD A POSTCRITICAL HERMENEUTICS

But then, faced with the crisis of meaning in our societies, what sort of managerial philosophy can we imagine, both in the educational field and on the more general level of the ecological and technological evolution of the contemporary world, if we start from the principle that establishing the relationship between philosophy and management necessarily leads us down the path of what we might call a "philosophy of management"?

It seems clear that the traditional tools and techniques of the discipline are no longer sufficient. The managerial vita activa, that which is likely to give rise to another framework and new horizons, requires an appropriate response to the automaticity of measurement and judgment, to increase our tolerance of uncertainty and, ultimately, rediscover our humanity in an increasingly robotized world: not by mobilizing new techniques, but by cultivating know-how, as a key ability capable of inspiring all the others. Indeed, reading is not a means of acquiring any kind of bookish wisdom or literary know-how. But to read to cultivate a mode of deciphering social relations in the service of an axiology no longer based solely on quantification and the—very real¯power of numbers, but to cultivate the Stoic (and Augustinian) "Ne quid nimis."[6]

Curiously enough, reading skills have been shown to be a formidable asset in the face of the pandemic, which upended life all over the world in that sad year. Confronted with this tragedy, we realized to what extent our society had become somewhat "nosocomial," in the sense that not only did we have to deal with COVID-19, but also with other pernicious infections such as fake news and conspiracy theories, whose proliferation and mutation can destroy social relations and produce any number of chaotic phenomena. If managers are soon to become "nurses of the organization," as Nietzsche wished philosophers to be the "doctors of civilization," this evolution will not take place without an essential period of diagnosis in which the ability to exercise judgment in an ethical and critical manner will have a central role to play. Faced with the hubris of certain leaders, the exclusive focus on calculability, and the rise of functional stupidity, this new breed of nurses will have to base their steering of organizations on what offers resistance to the virtualization of human relations and engages in a process of socialization that appears to be a necessary condition for any subjective development (and constitutes a refusal to let our feelings be formatted). Such an approach to management seeks to counteract the permanent tension of our thoughts by the sole means of calculation, relying on the notion of "professions" rather than "functions," to revalue the know-how and the acquired savoir-vivre in the long term. Fighting dehumanization is not just a matter of loudly proclaiming the centrality of women and men in the organizations, but rather of acting with benevolence, whether formal or more informal.[7]

To this end, it seems equally necessary to make room for the imagination of decision makers, not only for their power of constraint and their inclination to imitate,[8] to prevent them from becoming, without always being aware of it, "prisoners of agreed and ritualised forms of evaluation and judgement."[9] In management, one need to know how to interpret signals as well as orders. Winning organizations are those in which people know how to interpret orders before following them or not—for example, to deal with an unforeseen obstacle. I maintain, therefore, like many of the authors discussed in this book, and beyond their often very different if not opposing political sensibilities, that this qualitarism will not be able to do without critical reflection. But the meaning of this critique needs to be entirely revisited, because we must be able to formulate proposals that are neither bellicose nor marked with the seal of certainty (the one that drives you crazy, as Nietzsche points out), or even resentment, a phenomenon that is growing rapidly these days and has not entirely spared some of the authors included in this collection. Instead of this belligerence tinged with rancor, it would be more appropriate to experience the "gracious and loving kindness" that Dorian Astor evokes from a postcritical angle.[10]

At a time of great challenges and unparalleled environmental risks, a postcritical hermeneutics reminds us of the need to interpret what is happening to us, a need that is more vital than ever. Such a posture allows us to engage in language games in a generous (a true Pascalian would dare to use the word "charity," in the sense of benevolence, at this point) but not naive attempt to unfold new perspectives for organizations and new responses to the ethical, epistemic, and political issues of the present day. Striking up a dialogue between books, selecting and connecting texts in the hope of learning something, forms a kind of modus operandi. A "weak" method, no doubt, but one that asserts this weakness in the manner of Gianni Vattimo, another champion of interpretivism in philosophy, in an attempt to escape the violence inherent in domineering discourses of absolute objective truth (in particular metaphysics caught in the trap of contemporary nihilism).[11] "For Vattimo," as John

Caputo writes, "hermeneutics is the best alternative because it is the most loving,"[12] recalling here, without a doubt, Saint Augustine's first "erotic" hermeneutical principle—namely, that all texts should be interpreted according to a commandment of love.[13] Caputo also adds, as if to inform economic decision makers of the role they have to play in this interpretive and dialogical score, the following comment: "the business of life is to strain to hear what is addressing to us, to enter into a dialogue in which the worlds beckons and we respond. This response is accomplished not in empty talk but in action (subtilitas applicandi), not in a single act but in the curve our life cuts as we move through the world, in everything we think or do in life."[14]

A "weak" method that aims not to demystify, an enterprise most often based on an ideological—or even utopian, but always transcendent and overarching—position, but rather to heal and to care. This method is, therefore, less interested in any "reality of facts," which is always open to various interpretations that are more or less fair or open to criticism, or in a purely instrumental approach to the issues we are dealing with here—particularly in educational terms where the usefulness of the useless is essential to remember—than in the creation of a space for thought and reflexivity. A space as a means of combating the systemic stupidity of organizations, and as a means of rediscovering a sense of and love for the common world, and for life itself.

TACT, MEASUREMENT, AND PLAYFULNESS

In the face of chaotic phenomena of all kinds, it is important today no longer to hate or judge—in the moral sense—but to understand and perhaps love,[15] to make possible once again, to better rebuild what still deserves to be rebuilt. Animated by this desire, I propose here some exploratory elements for a possible philosophy of management whose contours could provisionally unfold around three notions.

The first would be the meaning of "tact": if management comes from the word manus, it means that above all else, good management means exhibiting delicacy and tact. In a recent scientific article, Martin Kornberger and his colleagues have shown that in crisis situations, such as during the influx of migrants in Vienna, when multiple organizations had to improvise and cooperate in a context of very limited rationality and strong pressure, only what they call the "logic of tact" proved to be effective and efficient.[16] This logic is defined by these authors as a dynamic interplay between the accumulated knowledge of the situation and the course of action, without one dominating the other. Tact is the way in which, when faced with unforeseen—and tragic, in this case—events, decisions are taken according to two modalities (which they borrow from Clausewitz): first, the glance, which allows one to scan and prioritize in the face of an immediate problem, to intuitively guess the right solutions by feeling them, rather than being the object and result of a calculation. Second, courage of spirit: here again there is no preestablished plan but, rather, care, therapy, and direction given, with determination and moderation, to a situation that requires an immediate response.

Kornberger and his coauthors point out that "the elements outlined in a logic of tact do not operate in a sequential mode; rather, this logic corresponds to a dynamic model in which the elements represent forces (centrifugal, centripetal) that balance each other: this model does not allow us to predict the final outcome, but it does offer a schema of the forces invested in the battle."[17] Clearly, tact is not just a polite way of confronting or solving organizational problems but an alternative model of meaning to those generally taught, which favor cognition over action (e.g., algorithmic thinking) or the reverse (e.g., following a predefined protocol). But it also includes, by definition, an adaptive capacity in relations with others, of restraint, of finesse, of appreciation, of measurement, in short, of subtlety. Subtilitas, among the notions highlighted in this book, must be understood as this spirit of finesse as opposed to the spirit of geometry to which Blaise Pascal referred, a manner of approaching working relationships with more elegance. It is also a way of escaping vulgarity, in favor of a certain modesty in human relations; a capacity for interpretation, to rediscover shared forms of savoir-vivre.

The second notion that could contribute greatly to such a philosophical project would be mesotês. In organizations, private or public, small or large, figures are never "self-evident." They always presuppose a prior—qualitative—measurement. Every figure, every computer program, therefore, requires an "enlightened use of the numbers."[18] Without this reading key, without this interrogative and critical modality, numbers are perceived as primary ontological entities, whereas they are originally only the symbol of abstract equivalences. As Robert Salais, for example, reminds us:[19]

> Strength is a matter of arithmetic ("5 is greater than 3") and lies in the fact that it is unquestionable for common sense. But this is just an appearance. The work of the "professionals of numbers" underlines that we should not stop there. The data displayed takes on meaning in and through their staging within the framework of governance mechanisms.

Yet, faced with the power of figures, what alternative interpretative power can we propose? Several authors invoke the idea of mesotês, a word by which they mean a form of competence, which would support the good life, the quality of life itself, and thus contradict the bad Chrematistic, which favors accumulation, gigantism, and bad taste. When he evokes the metron (the measure)—etymologically linked to the mesotê—Olivier Rey specifies that it is a question of finding harmony in things, of reconnecting with the right proportion, the fairest and most humane measure. If calculations, he warns us, can lead us to the idea of symmetry, only the metron is capable of conveying a balanced judgment. The rise of a managerial conception centered on numbers, on algorithmic governmentality, may also bring to mind the most striking intuitions of Günther Anders when he evoked the derealizing effect of numbers and the Promethean shame of the human being discharging responsibility by entrusting the machine with the power to decide.

In view of this observation, which Anders made as far back as 1956, I consider it preferable not to abandon hope too quickly in our human capacity for judgment—for "measuring," "weighing," and "feeling" people and situations—even though, and perhaps for this reason, too, it remains limited and unsatisfactory. This prerequisite seems to me infinitely preferable to any temptation to surrender our capacity for action,[20] either to the dashboards of governance by numbers, or to the calculations of algorithmic governmentality. The figure of the "weak" or "good enough"[21] manager—in reference to the "good enough mother" of psychoanalyst Donald Winnicott[22]—seems infinitely preferable to the replacement of our critical capacities by the sole power of algorithms.

Finally, we should bet on the potential for playfulness in professional relationships: this third element is close to what Pascal called "entertainment"—a word that is not only negative for him—namely, the ludic dimension as an antidote to the power of numbers. Playing with calculation, as a means of escaping from it, is an idea by several major thinkers in the sociology of work, including Marie-Anne Dujarier:[23]

> The workers collectively make a game from their prescribed task (painful and absurd), giving it a new meaning: it is no longer a question of moving metal plates but of beating speed scores . . . and above all, of inventing competitions with colleagues, in whose eyes it is possible to demonstrate one's virtuosity.

Ludicization, which I distinguish from the marketing processes of "gamification," would mean this: acting as if we were working while playing, and finally, reexamining our understanding of the relationship to work to prove Jean-Pierre Dupuy right[24] when he recalls Adam Smith's oft-cited maxim that the economy is, first and foremost, an "immense theatre where society tells stories about itself." The theatrical framework can lead to the emergence of new ways of doing things, new management models, the emergence of new forces within organizations, other than those strictly constituted by numbers and evaluation grids.[25]

Tact, a sense of measurement, and playfulness: these are the avenues of research that can contribute to a postcritical management,[26] inspired by the reading of the works I have reviewed in the joyful tradition of "philosophical distractions." They represent a humanistic countertrend to purely quantitative logic, through the acquisition of new skills—in the manner of martial arts, where practitioners must learn how to strike as well as how to parry a blow.

The real benefit of exploring these research avenues will be the opportunity to rediscover the meaning of desire in its proper, philosophical sense. This desire is also central to the economic reorientation of the present, as the possibility of an affective investment that seeks to sublimate our impulses in the long term, rather than constantly producing new ones in the short term. For, as the much-lamented Bernard Stiegler pointed out in a series of works, including one of his last essays, beautifully titled *Qu'appelle-t-on panser?*,[27] it is not consumption that we should seek to revive but desire—that is to say, an emotional and thoughtful investment to fight back against what he described as a generalized stupidification combined with symbolic misery.[28] We must commit ourselves to reinventing the "science" of management so that, as Husserl pointed out, it has something to tell us about ourselves, and that, reputed to be poor in meaning, it can reveal its own fruitfulness in our "noetic souls." With this goal in mind, the study of management must not shy away from confronting the broadest, most pressing issues facing our contemporary societies, whether it be the danger of cultural proletarianization, from within, or the outer threat of ecological ruin.

NOTES

1. See, for instance, G. Mercier and G. Deslandes, "There Are No Codes, Only Interpretations. Practical Wisdom and Hermeneutics in Monastic Organizations," *Journal of Business Ethics*, 2017.
2. J. Caputo, *Hermeneutics and Information. Facts and Interpretation of the Age of Information* (London: Pelican Book, 2018), cf. 112.
3. P. Ricoeur, *Du texte à l'action. Essais d'herméneutique*, t2 (Paris: Point, 1998).
4. R. Felski, *The Limites of Critique* (Chicago: University of Chicago Press, 2015), 2.
5. Quoted by J. Grondin, *L'herméneutique*. 5ème édition. Collection Que sais-je? (PUF, 2022), 104.
6. "Nothing too much," a Latin phrase suggested by Horace.
7. G. Mercier and G. Deslandes, "Formal and Informal Benevolence in a Profit-Oriented Context," *Journal of Business Ethics*, 2020.
8. G. Deslandes, *Critique de la condition managériale*, op. cit.
9. G. Julien and Y. Michaud, dir., *Mutation technologique et responsabilité humaine des dirigeants* (Paris: Odile Jacob, 2018), 74.
10. See G. Deslandes, *Poscritical Management Studies* (Springer, 2023).

11. G. Deslandes, "Weak Theology and Organization Studies," *Organization Studies 41*, no.1 (2018): 127–39.

12. Caputo, *Hermeneutics and Information*, 179.

13. G. Deslandes. *Érotique de l'administration* (PUF, 2023).

14. Caputo, *Hermeneutics and Information*, 310.

15. See G. Deslandes, *Erotique de l'administration* (PUF, 2023).

16. M. Kornberger, S. Leixnering, and R. Meyer, "The Logic of Tact: How Decisions Happen in Situations of Crisis," *Organization Studies 40*, no. 2 (2019): 239–66.

17. Ibid., 257.

18. In V. Charolles, "Facts and figures. Sur la mesure de la performance," *Le Débat,* 2016/5, n° 192, 100. doi: 10.3917/deba.192.0094. See also J. Muller, "The Costs of Accountability," *American Interest 11*, no. 1 (2015).

19. R. Salais, "Governance, Quantification and Law. About Alain Supiot, *Governance by numbers. Cours au Collège de France (2012–2014)*," *Revue Française de Socio-Économie 17* (2016): 187, doi: 10.3917/rfse.017.0185.

20. D. Cardon, *What Do Algorithms Dream of?* op. cit.

21. G. Deslandes, "Weak Theology and Organization Studies," *Organization Studies 41*, no. 1 (2018): 127–39.

22. Y. Michaud, *What Is Responsible Management? Confidence, Decision, Reflexivity* (Paris: Eyrolles, 2013).

23. M.-A. Dujarier, *Le Management désincarné* (Paris: La Découverte, 2015), with reference to the work of Donald Roy (*Un sociologue à l'usine*, La Découverte, 2006,) and Mickhaël Buravoy (*Produire le consentement*, La Ville brûle, 2015).

24. J.-P. Dupuy, *L'Avenir de l'économie. Sortir de l'écomystification* (Paris: Flammarion, 2012).

25. See S. Le Lay, «Des pratiques ouvrières ludiques aux dispositifs managériaux ludistes: vers une instrumentalisation du jeu dans le travail», *La nouvelle revue du travail 2* (2013), http://journals.openedition.org/nrt/702, doi: 10.4000/nrt.702.

26. G. Deslandes, *Postcritical Management Studies: Philosophical Investigations* (Dordrecht: Springer, 2023).

27. Paris, Les Liens qui Libèrent, 2018. See also G. Deslandes, L. Paltrinieri, L. "Entretien avec Bernard Stiegler," *Rue Descartes 91*, no. 1 (2017): 119–40.

28. B. Stiegler, *De la misère symbolique,* "Champs/essais," (Paris: Flammarion, 2013).

References

Alvesson, Mats, and Hugh Willmott, eds. *Studying Management Critically*. Londres: Sage, 2003.
Arena, Richard. "Adolphe-Jérôme Blanqui, 1798–1854. Un historien de l'économie aux préoccupations sociales." In Y. Breton and M. Lutfalla, eds., *L'économie politique en France au xixe siècle*. Paris: Economica, 1991.
Avolio, Bruce, and Bernard Bass. "Transformational Leadership, Charisma and Beyond." Working paper, State University of New York, Binghamton, 1985.
Babeau, Olivier, and Jean-François Chanlat. "La transgression, une dimension oubliée de l'organisation." *Revue française de gestion 183*, no. 3 (2008): 201–19. doi: 10.3166/rfg.183.201-219.
Bataille, Georges. "La notion de dépense." In *La Part maudite*. Paris: Minuit, 2014, 23–24.
Bouilloud, Jean-Philippe, and Ghislain Deslandes. "The Aesthetics of Leadership: Beau Geste as Critical Behaviour." *Organization Studies*, 2015.
Bourdieu, Pierre. *Les Règles de l'art*. Paris: Seuil, 1992, 162.
Bouveresse, Jacques. "Les managers peuvent-ils avoir un idéal?" In Essais, II., *L'époque, la mode, la morale, la satire*, 165–87. Marseille: Agone, 2001.
Carney, Brian, and Isaac Geetz. *Freedom, Inc.: How Corporate Liberation Unleashes Employee Potential and Business Performance*. Somme Valley House, 2016.
Cassin, Barbara. *Derrière les grilles. Sortons du tout-évaluation*. Mille et Une Nuits, 2014.
———. *Éloge de la traduction: compliquer l'universel*. Pluriel, 2022.
Chabot, Pascal. *Global Burn-out*. Paris: PUF, 2013.
Charolles, Valérie. "Facts and figures. Sur la mesure de la performance," *Le Débat*, 2016/5, n° 192, 100. doi: 10.3917/deba.192.0094. See also J. Muller, "The Costs of Accountability." *American Interest 11*, no. 1 (2015).
Deleuze, Gilles. "On the New Philosophers, and a More General Problem." In *Deux régimes de fous. Texts and Interviews 1975–1995*. Éditions de Minuit, 2003, 127–34.

Démier, François. "Blanqui, Adolphe (1798–1854). Professeur d'Économie industrielle (1834–1854)." In *Les professeurs du Conservatoire national des Arts et Métiers. Dictionnaire biographique*, 1794–1955, vol. 1: A–K. Paris: Institut national de Recherche pédagogique (INRP), 1994, 185–94.

Deneault, Alain. *Mediocracy: The Politics of the Extreme Centre*, trans. Catherine Brown. Between the Lines, 2018.

Deslandes, Ghislain. "Philosophy and Management Sciences: Towards a Poetics of Managerial Action? Orientation de recherche et questions d'enseignement." *Diotime 51*, no. 1 (2012).

———. *Critique de la condition managériale*. Paris: PUF, 2016.

———. "Weak Theology and Organization Studies." *Organization Studies 41*, no. 1 (2018): 127–39.

———. "European Management Teaching and Research: Reflections on the Life and Work of A. Blanqui." *European Management Journal 38*, no. 3 (June 2020): 357–66.

———. *Postcritical Management Studies: Philosophical Investigations*. Dordrecht: Springer, 2023.

Deslandes, Ghislain, and Jean-Philippe Bouilloud. "De quoi notre métier est-il le nom? Perspectives pour un débat." *Revue française de gestion 309*, no. 2 (2023): 85–99.

Deslandes, Ghislain, and Luca Paltrinieri. "Entretien avec Bernard Stiegler." *Rue Descartes 91*, no. 1 (2017): 119–40.

Dujarier, Marie-Anne. *Le Management désincarné*. Paris : La Découverte, 2015, with reference to the work of Donald Roy (2006, Un sociologue à l'usine, La Découverte) and Mickhaël Buravoy (2015, Produire le consentement, La Ville brûle).

Dupuy, Jean-Pierre. *L'Avenir de l'économie. Sortir de l'écomystification*. Paris: Flammarion, 2012.

Felski, Rita. *The Limites of Critique*. Chicago: University of Chicago Press, 2015.

Frey, Daniel. *L'Interprétation et la lecture chez Ricoeur et Gadamer*. Paris: PUF, 2008.

Gadamer, Hans. *Truth and method*. Bloomsbury, 2013.

Gorz, André. *Métamorphoses du travail : quête du sens*. Paris: Galilée, 1988, 141–42.

Grésin, Julien, and Yves Michaud, dir. *Mutation technologique et responsabilité humaine des dirigeants*. Paris: Odile Jacob, 2018, 74.

Grondin, Jean. *L'herméneutique*. 5ème édition. Collection Que sais-je? Paris: PUF, 2022.

Hardin, Garrett. *The Tragedy of the Commons*, trans. Laurent Bury, ed. and commentary Dominique Bourg. Paris: PUF, 2018.

Jankélévitch, Vladimir. *L'aventure, l'ennui, le sérieux*, text presented by Arnaud Sorosina. Paris: Flammarion, 2017–2018. This book is reviewed hereunder, cf. 55.

Juët, Rémi. *The Manager's Toolbox. 50 Practical Sheets for Managing Your Team*, third edition. Paris: Dunod, 2017.

Kierkegaard, Sören. Etapes sur les chemins de la vie. *Editions de l'Orant*e, 9 (1966).

Kornberger, Martin, Stepha Leixnering, and Renate Meyer. "The Logic of Tact: How Decisions Happen in Situations of Crisis." *Organization Studies 40*, no. 2 (2019): 239–66.

Lecourt, Dominique. "Pourquoi enseigner la philosophie et l'histoire de sciences dans les cursus scientifiques." *Rue Descartes 41*, no. 3 (2003): 105–8. doi :10.3917/rdes.041.0105.

Le Lay, Stéphane. (2013). "Des pratiques ouvrières ludiques aux dispositifs managériaux ludistes: vers une instrumentalisation du jeu dans le travail." *La nouvelle revue du travail,* 2, 2013. http://journals.openedition.org/nrt/702. doi: 10.4000/nrt.702.

McLuhan, Marshall. *Pour comprendre les médias.* Paris: Seuil, 1968, 88.

Mercier, Guillaume, and Ghislain Deslandes. "There Are No Codes, Only Interpretations. Practical Wisdom and Hermeneutics in Monastic Organizations." *Journal of Business Ethics 145* (2017): 781–94.

———. "Formal and Informal Benevolence in a Profit-Oriented Context." *Journal of Business Ethics 165*, no. 1 (2020): 125–43.

Michaud, Yves. *What Is Responsible Management? Confidence, Decision, Reflexivity.* Paris: Eyrolles, 2013.

Pearce, Craig, and Jay Conger. *Shared Leadership: Reframing the Hows and Whys of Leadership.* Thousand Oaks, CA: Sage, 2003.

Péguy, Charles. Pensées, 1934, in Œuvres complètes, tome 1. Paris, Gallimard, "Bibliothèque de la Pléiade," 1986, 1103.

Renouard, Alfred. *History of the Ecole Supérieure de Commerce (1820–1898).* Union amicale des anciens élèves, 79 Avenue de la République, Paris, 1898.

Ricoeur, Paul. *Du texte à l'action. Essais d'herméneutique*, t2 (Paris: Point, 1998).

Salais, Robert. "Governance, Quantification and Law. About Alain Supiot, Governance by Numbers. Cours au Collège de France (2012–2014)." *Revue Française de Socio-Économie*, 17 (2016): 187. doi: 10.3917/rfse.017.0185.

Supiot, Alain. *Governance by numbers. Courses at the Collège de France, 2012–2014*, Institut d'Études avancées de Nantes/Fayard, 2015.

Uhl-Bien, Mary. "Relational Leadership and Gender: From Hierarchy to Relationality." In P. Werhane and M. Painter-Morland, eds., *Leadership, Gender and Organization*, Dordrecht: Springer, 2011.

Name Index

Subject Index

About the Author

Ghislain Deslandes is professor at ESCP Business School (Paris Campus), in the Law, Economics and Humanities Department (LEH). His teaching and research activities focus on continental philosophy and management studies. His most recent research has been published in journals such as *Journal of Business Ethics*, *Leadership*, *Management Learning*, *Organization*, and *Organization Studies*. He has published a dozen books, most recently *Post-critical Management Studies: Philosophical Investigations*. A former program director at the Collège International de Philosophie (CIPh), he is also the author of various philosophical articles and essays, such as *Antiphilosophy of Christianity* and *The Idea of Beginning in Jules Lequier's Philosophy*.

www.ingramcontent.com/pod-product-compliance
Ingram Content Group UK Ltd.
Pitfield, Milton Keynes, MK11 3LW, UK
UKHW041839031026
15587UKWH00002B/869

9 781666 961720